1217

MORALITY,
LAW AND GRACE

J. N. D. ANDERSON, O.B.E., LL.D., F.B.A.

*Professor of Oriental Laws, and Director of the
Institute of Advanced Legal Studies, in the University of London*

TYNDALE PRESS
39 BEDFORD SQUARE, LONDON WC1B 3EY

© THE TYNDALE PRESS

First Edition January 1972

INTERNATIONAL STANDARD BOOK NUMBERS:
PAPERBACK 0 85111 308 7
LIBRARY EDITION 0 85111 728 7

*Printed and bound in Great Britain by
Billing & Sons Limited, Guildford and London*

CONTENTS

PREFACE

The genesis of this book was the Forwood Lectures on the Philosophy and History of Religion which I was invited to give in the University of Liverpool in February 1971. I am most grateful to the Dean of the Faculty of Arts, and the Committee over which he presides, for the honour of this invitation and for all the kindness and hospitality they showed me. Chapters 2, 3 and 5 represent, with only minimal amendments, the lectures I gave on that occasion.

Since then, I have added chapters 4 and 1. The former continues, in a sense, the subject of chapter 3 – 'Morality and Law' – but turns from 'General considerations' to the special problem of 'Tyranny and injustice'. This is clearly a question of vital – and even urgent – importance today. Finally, I added an introductory chapter on 'Morality and Determinism', since it seemed to me essential to give some consideration, however cursory, to the basic problem of how far we are in fact responsible for our moral decisions and behaviour.

The fact that this book is based on a short series of three lectures, expanded only to the extent mentioned above, will perhaps explain why a vast range of subjects, which would have demanded detailed consideration in any textbook on morality, has received only the most scanty mention, or even no mention at all, in these pages. In my second chapter, for example, I have tried to show how ambivalent our contemporary attitude is to many matters of both private and social morality. But far from criticizing the fervour with which many of the younger generation crusade today against the evils of racial discrimination, crushing poverty (in spite of all that the Welfare State has achieved), social injustice and international exploitation (whether physical, psychological or economic), I heartily commend it. Much more, not less, needs to be done in this wide field of public morality. Yet it would be a mistake to let these urgent considerations blind our eyes to the problems of private morality which concern us all. Here we are not faced with a question of 'either . . . or' but of 'both . . . and'.

The reason why a somewhat disproportionate part of that chapter is, moreover, concerned with matters of sex is not that I think that the church, or the individual Christian, should be obsessed with this subject to the exclusion of other matters of urgent public concern, but because it is precisely at this point that our contemporary society may most justly be described as 'permissive'. Had space permitted, other points of personal morality – such as financial 'fiddling', petty theft, slip-shod work, restrictive practices and arrant unconcern for the welfare of society as a whole – would also have been discussed. But perhaps the inclusion of chapter 4, with its emphasis on those social, economic and racial injustices which can all too easily reach intolerable proportions, may serve in some measure to adjust the balance.

I am much indebted to several friends who have been kind enough to read parts of this book in manuscript and give me the benefit of their criticisms and advice. Professor Eric Mascall was good enough to read it all; Dr Martyn Lloyd-Jones chapters 1 and 4; Professor Richard Field chapter 3; and Professors Robert Boyd, Malcolm Jeeves, Donald MacKay, John Marsh and Desmond Pond all, or part, of chapter 1. I am most grateful for their kindness and helpful comments, but must, of course, exonerate them from any responsibility for the book in its final form.

1 MORALITY AND DETERMINISM

The subject of morality and determinism has received such a vast amount of expert attention that it may seem presumptuous and unnecessary to devote one short chapter in a book like this to so complex and profound a problem. But it seems to me unrealistic to publish a book, however slim, which is largely devoted to morality – and morality in relation to both law and grace – without some preliminary discussion of the basic question whether human beings do, in fact, enjoy any real freedom of moral choice or whether their reactions to every situation and challenge are 'inevitable' and 'unavoidable'. We all realize, of course, that we can often forecast how we ourselves, or those we know best, are exceedingly likely to react in certain circumstances; for we are clearly, to some extent, pre-conditioned by our temperament, by our memory (conscious and subconscious) of past experiences, and by our training and environment to respond in a predictable way to given stimuli. Yet we all, I think, have the instinctive feeling, however mistaken this may conceivably be, that we enjoy a genuine, though limited, freedom of choice in the detailed conduct of our daily lives.

We are uncertain whether to catch the 8.30 or the 9.30 train, and it is not until 7.45 that we finally make up our minds. The decision we reach is, no doubt, influenced by our inherent laziness, on the one hand, or by our instinctive preference for getting on with things, on the other. It may also be affected by the weather, by the state of our health, by the apparently fortuitous circumstances of a telephone call, or by a hundred and one other factors. Yet we are often con-

vinced that the final decision was in fact our own, and sometimes that it was a touch-and-go affair; and we suffer from the
illusion, at least, that we might easily have reached the opposite decision.

Precisely the same applies to the major decisions of life:
what career we choose, whether (and whom) we marry,
where we live. No doubt most of us are fitted by temperament,
ability and taste for one type of job rather than another;
and this is one reason why expert advice is available – and
often valuable – to help us make a realistic assessment. But
it is an undeniable fact that we often look back and feel convinced that we made a foolish mistake even in so fundamental
a choice. Again, it is clear that some people inherit – or,
more likely, acquire in early childhood – such psychological
fixations or homosexual tendencies that, for them, a normal
marriage may be out of the question. But it is equally clear
that, to all appearances at least, most of us enjoy a considerable latitude of choice as to whether to marry or remain
single, whether to propose to X or to accept the proposal of
Y – and that we are sometimes wise, and sometimes sadly
mistaken, in the decision we make.

It is obvious, moreover, even from this very surface consideration of the problem, that we cannot confine our attention
to a single individual in complete isolation. Even if it were
arguable that the genes Mary or John may inherit, or the
chemical composition of their brains, inevitably decree the
sort of persons they will turn out to be, the decisions that make
up their lives will not be reached in isolation but in the interplay of relationships with other people and in the context of a
multitude of apparently fortuitous circumstances. So a con-
sistent philosophy of determinism must go well beyond the
individual and embrace the whole world in which we live,
material, psychological and spiritual.

But this is a philosophy of life which it is very difficult, to
say the least, to maintain consistently and to defend convinc-
ingly in practice. A friend of mine who is a convinced determinist, for example, has written an excellent little book on how
students should set out on the study of the subject he professes
so ably (what habits and attitudes of mind they should seek

to develop, how they should learn to use a library, what sort of notes they should make, *etc.*). Elsewhere, however, he tells us that 'on a determinist view every impulse, if in fact not resisted, was in those circumstances irresistible. A so-called irresistible impulse is simply one in which the desire to perform a particular act is not influenced by other factors.' Thus the only justification for promulgating criminal laws, for example, is that 'for mankind in the mass it is impossible to tell whom the threat of punishment will restrain and whom it will not. For most it will succeed; for some it will fail, and the punishment must then be applied to these criminals in order to maintain the threat for persons generally.'[1] So we must, presumably, conclude that it was because of an irresistible impulse that he wrote his book; that the existence of this book, and the admirable advice it contains, must be regarded as one factor in evoking in some students an irresistible impulse to study effectively, although in other cases it will inevitably fail in its purpose; and that the students concerned have no real liberty of choice whether to be industrious or idle, systematic or slipshod – or, indeed, whether to choose to read this book at all, should circumstances, or some well-meaning friend, ever bring it to their attention.

Precisely the same sort of considerations apply to the more obviously moral decisions of life. We can readily concede, for example, that A grows up with a sexual urge, whether normal or deviant, which makes him particularly vulnerable to temptations from which another man is comparatively free; that B has a proclivity to be untruthful or dishonest in a way which would scarcely occur to someone else; and that there are infinite varieties of 'diminished moral responsibility'. But is it really impossible, for anyone who is not an infant or radically abnormal, to make *any* moral choice which is other than 'inevitable', however limited his options may be? Are we utterly incapable of coming to a 'free', or even comparatively free, decision as to what we read, where we go, what friends we make, and whether we flirt with (or try to resist) the temptations to which we know we are prone?

[1] Glanville L. Williams, *The Criminal Law* (Stevens, London, 1953), pp. 346 f.

Must we not concede – whether thankfully or grudgingly – that we have in fact a measure, at least, of moral responsibility?

IS DETERMINISM SYNONYMOUS WITH FATALISM?

It may, of course, be argued that determinism is not necessarily synonymous with fatalism. The distinction which is sometimes made is that the determinist believes that there are certain causal laws which are universally true and which in given circumstances (that is, where the possible variables are the same) will always produce the same result. The fatalist, on the other hand, goes so far as to assert that the efforts we make will have no effect whatever on the end product. And this, it is asserted, 'is a stronger claim than determinism, in effect not only claiming that our outputs are caused, but also specifying certain factors as being causally irrelevant to the outcome'.[1] But in point of fact it is exceedingly difficult to distinguish the two in practice. This may be vividly illustrated, in the context of this book, by a few sentences from an address once delivered by a well-known American lawyer to the inmates of a prison, when he said: 'There is no such thing as a crime as the word is generally understood. I do not believe there is any sort of distinction between the real moral conditions of the people in and out of jail. One is as good as the other. The people here can no more help being in here than the people outside can avoid being outside. I do not believe that people are in jail because they deserve to be. They are in jail simply because they cannot avoid it on account of circumstances which are entirely beyond their control and for which they are in no sense responsible.' Then, referring to a list of crimes, he continued: 'There are a great many people here who have done some of these things who really do not know why they did them. It looked to you at the time as if you had a chance to do them or not, as you saw fit; but still, after all you had no choice. . . . You could not help it any more than we outside can help taking the positions that we take.'[2]

---

[1] *Determinism, Free Will and Moral Responsibility*, edited by Gerald Dworkin (Prentice-Hall, New Jersey, 1970), pp. 3 and 4.
[2] Clarence Darrow in Cook County Jail, as quoted in Dworkin, *op. cit.*, p. 1.

To put the same point in a much less extreme form, the doctrine of determinism has been defined by one of its more moderate advocates as 'the view that every event A is so connected with a later event B that, given A, B must occur. By indeterminism I mean the view that there is some event B that is not so connected with any previous event A that, given A, it must occur'.[1] And the only concession this writer makes to the instinctive feeling almost all of us have that we can sometimes, at least, do as we choose is to backdate the determinism to the choice rather than the action (*i.e.* to postulate that we can, indeed, do as we choose, but we cannot choose as we would). But is this argument always and invariably valid?

There are at least four planes on which the debate between the exponents of determinism and those of a certain freedom of moral choice normally pursue their argument: that of the physicist, the psychologist, the philosopher and the theologian. Unhappily, I have no expertise in any one of these four disciplines, so it is no doubt foolhardy to tackle the problem at all. But many of those who read this book may not have had any training in science, psychology, philosophy or theology, and very few will have any real knowledge of more than one of them. It may be of some value, therefore, for a self-confessed amateur to attempt to outline, in simple terms, some of the considerations involved. But we must frankly recognize that this whole subject constitutes one of the most insoluble mysteries of life, and that it would be foolish in the extreme to imagine that we can do more than make a few tentative suggestions as to how it may, perhaps, be approached. It must, inevitably, remain a paradox, and a paradox which comprises much that is obscure. I have myself spent hours discussing some of the relevant arguments (particularly in regard to what I have termed 'the physical approach') with the experts whose views I have summarized; and I still find one of these arguments singularly elusive. It may well be that some readers would find it more profitable, therefore, to postpone trying to thread their way through the more intricate

[1] *Determinism and Freedom in the Age of Modern Science*, edited by Sidney Hook (New York University Press, 1958), p. 4.

by-ways of this particular problem until they have first traversed the much more open ground over which the highway of my subject pursues its course.

We will start with the physical approach, because it is, in one sense, the simplest and most straightforward. This is, of course, a brash statement, since I must confess at once that the argument usually moves on a scientific plane which is well above my head. Its simplicity consists in the fact that it concentrates, essentially, on a single individual and concerns itself with the physical condition of his brain. It is this alone, some physiologists maintain, which will determine what he will remember or forget, what he will consider important or irrelevant, what urges he will experience and how he will respond to them. There can be no doubt, moreover, that a strong case can be made out for this point of view. The treatment of what is now called 'chemical depression', for example, has been revolutionized by an ever-increasing knowledge of the effects of a whole plethora of drugs on the feelings and moods we experience, the way in which we think, the very attitude to life which we adopt. Somewhat similarly, the injection or extraction of certain hormones can not only influence sexual urges and habits, but produce profound changes in the outward form, at least, that our very personality assumes. And precisely the same can be said about the effects of surgical operations. It might well be argued, therefore, that when we speak about the mind of man as largely controlling his behaviour, what we really mean is that the actual cells of his brain, in a material sense, and the mechanics of the way in which they operate and respond to stimuli, provide (had we the necessary knowledge) the all-sufficient explanation of how his 'mind' works and how his 'personality' develops. In the final analysis every conundrum, on this view, should be open to solution by the microscope, or by other scientific examination of a basically physical nature.

Another (but much less contemporary) school of thought takes what may be said to be the diametrically opposite point of view regarding the relationship between 'mind' and 'brain'. In the mind of man, its proponents would maintain, there is something over and beyond the cells which constitute the physical make-up of his cerebrum. Indeed, the relationship between mind and brain has even been compared with a violinist and the instrument on which he plays. On this view it is the decisions a man makes and the things he believes which produce continual changes in the chemical composition of his brain cells. As an extreme example some would cite the extraordinary feats performed by certain Hindu yogis, Muslim dervishes or Christian ascetics as a result of the exacting régime of mental and physical discipline to which they have deliberately devoted themselves. But the same point can also be made about much more ordinary people in the normal course of their everyday lives. Yet the fact remains that it is only through the instrumentality of the brain that any one of us can decide to devote himself to some course of action or discipline of thought.

How, then, can this apparent polarization be reconciled? Only, it would seem, by recognizing that there is a sense in which both are true: that the chemical composition of the brain has an enormous influence on the way in which the mind works and the man behaves, and that every decision he takes begets a corresponding chain-reaction in the chemical constitution of his brain. In other words we are looking at the same phenomenon from two different angles, and the individual concerned cannot be explained on an exclusively physical nor an exclusively mental, psychological or spiritual basis. On the contrary, there exists what may be termed a two-way relationship, although the physical and the other-than-physical can in no sense be regarded as independent entities, since a human being is essentially a unity. Put in yet another way, the Christian would confidently affirm, with E. L. Mascall, that all human experience takes upon itself a double character, spirituality and materiality, 'for we live in the borderland where matter is raised to the level of spirit and spirit immerses itself in matter. . . . Man is thus on the frontier where matter impinges upon spirit and itself becomes spiritualised, not by losing its own materiality but by becoming one organism with the spirit which assumes it, that bipartite organism of body and soul which is called man.'[1] It is possible, of course, to confine our attention either to the cells of a man's brain or to the cognitive processes of his mind; but these are, in fact, two aspects of a complex whole. It is this, indeed, which explains why the treatment of psychosomatic conditions may concentrate on either the physical or the psychological manifestations or causes of the patient's disorder.

Numerous illustrations can be given of the relationship between what we may designate as brain and mind. Thus an expert in phonetics and linguistics who tape-records a conversation between two friends may be able to analyse the phonetic, and even the linguistic, structure of the language they used without having any knowledge whatever of the meaning of what they said. Indeed, he might be able to do this with admirable accuracy even if he had reason to doubt whether the sounds they made, or the sentences they put together, had any meaning whatever. Similarly, a man who understood the meaning of what they said could analyse the substance of their conversation in spite of the fact that he had no knowledge whatever of the phonetic or linguistic structure of the language concerned. Yet certain changes, at least, in the sounds they made, or the order in which they made them, would inevitably entail a change in the substance of their conversation; and any alteration in the substance of what they said would inevitably necessitate a corresponding alteration in the words or sentences they used, or at least in their intonation. Thus the physical manifestations of speech and the meaning it is intended to convey may be distinguished but cannot be divided; they are two distinct, but in no real sense independent, aspects of one complex whole.

The relevance of this to our problem is, I think, obvious. If a man's reactions and behaviour were determined exclusively by the chemical composition of his brain, and by how that brain responds to the various stimuli of circumstances and human relationships, then the physiological case for mechanistic determinism might, perhaps, be regarded as proved. In reality, however, this is an inadequate and one-

[1] E. L. Mascall, *The Importance of Being Human* (Columbia University Press, New York, 1958), pp. 34 f.

sided view, for it ignores the other aspect of the whole phenomenon. Indeed, D. M. MacKay has argued[1] that, even on
the most mechanistic view of this matter, should some 'Super-
scientist' be able, with the help of instruments far more sophisticated than any yet invented, to read every detail of the cellular activity of a man's brain at a time when he was still
uncertain whether to catch the 8.30 or 9.30 train (to go back
to one of our previous examples), and thereby to predict to
his own satisfaction what decision the man concerned would
eventually reach, this assessment and prediction could have
no validity for the would-be traveller himself – because, had
he come to know the scientist's prediction and accepted its
accuracy, this act of cognition would, of itself, have effected
vital changes in his brain cells. So, the argument runs, the
traveller's belief that the outcome was still indeterminate up to
7.45 cannot be refuted, but is in fact confirmed, on the most
mechanistic theory of cellular activity. The decision he reaches
at 7.45 will certainly *coincide* with a cellular change, but it
would make no more sense to assert that the decision was
'caused' by the change in his brain than to affirm that the
activity of his brain cells was 'caused' by his decision. The idea
of causality is, in point of fact, inappropriate here, and it
would be much more meaningful to say that the two aspects
of what took place – the decision and the change in his brain
cells at the moment when that decision was reached – reflect
a unity which includes or embodies both.

It follows that the description the man himself would give
of the way in which he made up his mind, and the description the scientist would give of his brain's cellular activity,
would both be correct – but viewed, of course, from essentially
different standpoints. In other words, what might conceivably
be predicted with precision by a scientist from outside, and
even guessed by the man himself (on the basis of such knowledge of his own character and circumstances as he may have)
from inside, could not possibly be foretold with certainty
in terms which are inevitable or meaningful for the man him-

---

[1] *Cf.* 'Man as a Mechanism', in *Christianity in a Mechanistic Universe* (Inter-
Varsity Press, London, 1965), *Freedom of Action in a Mechanistic Universe*
(Cambridge University Press, London, 1967), and elsewhere.

self at the time when he has not yet made his decision; so his freedom of moral choice, within limits, remains unimpaired.

This is one of the points where a clear-cut distinction must be made between inanimate objects, on the one hand, and human beings (or, to a limited extent, any sentient creature), on the other. If scientific evidence is available that there will be an eclipse of the moon next week and A does not believe this, then A will clearly be deluded; for the eclipse of the moon is not in any way dependent on A's knowledge or belief. But should a Super-scientist ever be able so to read and interpret the condition of A's brain cells as to predict secretly, with hypothetical certainty, what decision he will reach next week about some matter regarding which he has not yet made up his mind, A would not, in fact, be under any illusion if he continued to believe that the decision he still has to take remains an 'open' one, for there is no possible way in which the scientist's secret prediction could have what MacKay terms 'a demonstrable claim to A's unconditional assent'. In order that A should believe the scientist's prediction, his brain cells would have to undergo such a change that the whole basis of the prediction would be vitiated. To put it in other words, this means that a prediction of what will happen in the future in regard to inanimate bodies may have an objective claim to universal acceptance, but that a prediction of what a sentient and cognitive human being will in the future decide to believe or do cannot have the same claim to represent objective truth for all the parties concerned, since it may well have no claim to the unconditional assent of the person himself. For him, at least, his future decision is still, in this sense, 'free'; and this must be true not only for the man himself but also for all other persons who remain in dialogue or any other reciprocal relationship with him.[1]

[1] In MacKay's own words, this means 'that where beliefs about the future of cognitive agents are concerned, the correctness, inevitability, *etc.*, of what is believed may (and in certain cases *must*) depend in a non-trivial way upon *who believes it*. The relativistic question thus thrust upon us is merely begged, and not answered, by the bland use of expressions such as "in fact" to introduce the observers'-eye-view of A's future, as if it had some accepted logical claim to be the "real truth" over against A's view . . .

This argument is designed to show that, even on the most mechanistic view of the cellular activity of the human brain, someone who has not yet taken a decision is not deluded in his conviction that certain options are still open to him. But it is far from clear that an extreme mechanistic view is empirically correct. Thus Nathaniel Micklem, describing the dilemma he faces when he has to make moral decisions between what he would like to do and what he feels he probably ought to do, writes that an electroencephalographic machine 'would doubtlessly record all the movements of my brain as I painfully come to my decisions; the brain may record *my* thoughts and *my* emotional struggles, but to suppose that the cerebral mass inside my skull does the thinking and deciding, while I, who think I am deciding, am a mere automaton, seems very great nonsense. If I really *believed* that I am a mere automaton, I should not wrestle with my conscience; I should merely wait to see what happened! But, even so, *I* should wait to see; there is no getting away from "*I*". . . . If I cannot remember a name or a word that eludes me, I "cudgel my brains" to find it. If I would write an essay I must use my brains; it is not really sense in this case to think of my brains using me and creating the mind, the "me" that they are using.'[1]

In point of fact, it seems that most biological scientists have, in recent years, largely abandoned any simple concept of rigid chains of causation. Today they tend to think more in terms of theories of probability, much as physicists have been doing for some time. A plausible psychophysiological formulation of the situation, when a human being subjectively perceives that he is confronted with the possibility of choice, is – I am told[2] – that there are active in his brain a number of possible programmes of action which 'are of equal potential

---

His subjective feeling of freedom rests on the proposition (which the observers can confirm) that until he makes up his mind no complete prediction of his brain-state exists with an unconditional, take-it-or-leave-it logical claim to *his* assent, or, indeed, to the assent of anyone potentially in dialogue with him' ('Choice in a Mechanistic Universe?', in *British Journal of the Philosophy of Science*, Sept. 1971).

[1] N. Micklem, *The Art of Thought* (London, Epworth Press, 1970), pp. 17 f.
[2] By my friend Dr Desmond Pond, Professor of Psychiatry at the London Hospital.

or valency', having regard to the stimuli to which he is subject at the time. This means, presumably, that the most one can postulate regarding the decision to which he will eventually come is in terms of what is probable. But the inadequacy of an extreme mechanistic view is particularly clear when, as is so often the case, this view is itself based on a naturalistic conception of the universe, according to which there is no Supernatural Being in control but everything is governed, down to the smallest detail, by physical laws. The difficulty in accepting this view may in part, perhaps, be illustrated by the case of a man, wrestling with some acute problem, who feels much inclined to take a certain decision but still hesitates, and whose friends then persuade him to stake the issue on the toss of a coin or the drawing of lots. Here it might be possible in theory, as it seems to me, for a Super-scientist so to have read the cellular condition of his brain as to predict the decision he felt inclined to take, the hesitation to which he was, perhaps, naturally prone, and even – conceivably – the likelihood that he would accept the suggestion that he should commit the issue to chance; but *not* the final outcome. The decision which resulted from his resort to coin or lot might well, in point of fact, have been one which was *contrary* to the way in which his brain was previously working, or to which his character would naturally have inclined.

Again, it seems exceedingly difficult to reconcile an extreme mechanistic view with the exercise of rational thought. If the workings of every man's mind are exclusively determined by the mechanics of his brain, then how can it be shown that one man's view is correct and another's mistaken? How, indeed, can the most convinced determinist defend his philosophy of life? In J. B. S. Haldane's words: 'If my mental processes are determined wholly by the motions of the atoms in my brain, I have no reason to suppose that my beliefs are true . . . and hence I have no reason for supposing my brain to be composed of atoms.'[1]

All knowledge, in other words, depends on the interplay of reason and experience. Thus C. S. Lewis insists that 'If the

[1] J. B. S. Haldane, *Possible Worlds* (Chatto and Windus, London, 1945 edition), p. 209.

feeling of certainty which we express by words like *must be* and *therefore* and *since* is a real perception of how things outside our own minds really "must" be, well and good. But if this certainty is merely a feeling *in* our own minds and not a genuine insight into realities beyond them – if it merely represents the way our minds happen to work – then we can have no knowledge. Unless human reasoning is valid no science can be true.'[1] Equally, of course, the most logical thought will inevitably lead to false conclusions if it starts from incorrect premises. But on a totally mechanistic theory, 'the finest piece of scientific reasoning is caused in just the same irrational way as the thoughts a man has because a bit of bone is pressing on his brain'. This does not make sense.

THE PSYCHOLOGICAL APPROACH

So much for the physical approach to this problem, some of which moves in realms of scientific fact and fantasy in which I find myself singularly alien and ill at ease. Much the same also applies in part, of course, to the psychological approach, which poses the question whether a man's every action is so governed by the genes he has inherited, and by those traits of character and conscious or sub-conscious motivation inbred in him by the experiences of infancy and early childhood, that he cannot in any real sense be held to be a morally responsible agent. Nor am I in any way competent to judge how far this approach coincides with the physiological; for presumably all a man's past experiences and present inclinations have affected, and continue to affect, his brain cells in a way which would, in terms of a theory which borders on the fantastic, be open to scientific scrutiny. But, however that may be, we here come to a significant difference in emphasis.

In this realm of ideas a lawyer is, superficially at least, somewhat more at home. Every system of criminal law recognizes that there are circumstances in which a man should not be held responsible for his actions, and others in which his responsibility is at least mitigated. Examples which spring to mind are acts done when a man is unconscious, when he is fundamentally mistaken about what he is doing, when he is

[1] C. S. Lewis, *Miracles* (Fontana, London, 1967 edition), p. 18.

the victim of gross coercion or when he suffers from certain
types of mental disease, brain damage or glandular deficiency.[1]
But the problem goes much deeper than this; and it has been
plausibly argued that there are many other cases in which a
man cannot justly be held responsible for his actions. As John
Hospers puts it: 'The deed may be planned, it may be carried
out in cold calculation, it may spring from the agent's character and be continuous with the rest of his behavior, and it
may be perfectly true that he could have done differently *if*
he had wanted to; nonetheless his behavior was brought
about by unconscious conflicts developed in infancy, over
which he had no control and of which (without training in
psychiatry) he does not even have knowledge. He may even
think he knows why he acted as he did, he may *think* he has
conscious control over his actions, he may even *think* he is
fully responsible for them; but he is not. Psychiatric casebooks
provide hundreds of examples . . . Countless criminal acts are
thought out in great detail; yet the participants are (without
their own knowledge) acting out fantasies, fears, and defenses
from early childhood, over whose coming and going they have
no conscious control.'[2]

Elsewhere, however, the same writer observes: 'I am only
saying that frequently persons we think responsible are not
properly to be called so; we mistakenly think them responsible
because we assume they are like those in whom no unconscious
drive (towards this type of behavior) is present, and that their
behavior can be changed by reasoning, exhorting or threatening.' In other words, some people cannot be held responsible
for compulsive actions (if any) which are exclusively the 'inevitable consequences' of situations in which, in infancy,
they were 'passive victims'.[3] This can, I think, be readily
accepted. But he pertinently adds that psychiatrists and psy-
choanalysts affirm that 'actions fulfilling this description are
characteristic of all people some of the time and some people
most of the time'.[4] This means, presumably, that most

---

[1] Some of which are, of course, perfectly susceptible to surgical, chemical or
psychiatric treatment.
[2] *Determinism and Freedom,* edited by Sidney Hook, p. 114.
[3] *Ibid.,* p. 118.   [4] *Ibid.*

of us act in the way we do – in many cases, at least – because we so choose; that we make this choice for a variety of different reasons, but chiefly in accordance with what we commonly call our 'character'; and that our character, in its turn, is in large part determined by genes, temperament, past experiences, *etc.*, over which we have little or no control.

Yet it is only an extremely doctrinaire determinist who would maintain that every thought most of us think, every word we speak, and every act we do is the inevitable and unavoidable expression of forces which are entirely beyond our own control. There is very strong evidence, as I see it, for believing that we are often subject to influences which suggest but do not constrain; that there are many occasions on which the choice we make is influenced, no doubt, but not finally determined by our character. And each such act or choice is itself, inevitably, a component in the character which will, in turn, influence our future actions. There is a fundamental difference between asserting that an action is 'causally determined', on the one hand, and 'inevitable' and 'unavoidable', on the other. No doubt it is necessary for a man to make a clear-cut choice and effort of the will if he is to overcome the down-drag of heredity or of inbred tendencies acquired in infancy; and it may readily be accepted that the very ability to make this effort is itself present or absent, in varying degrees, in different persons. Spinoza was clearly right, moreover, when he said that the only thing that can overcome a desire is a stronger contrary desire. But desires do not come exclusively from inside; they may well be awakened, fostered and strengthened from outside, too. And what evidence can, in fact, be adduced that the man concerned is always and completely the slave of inward tendencies and outward influences – that he is in no sense whatever a 'free' agent in what he chooses and what he does?

As C. A. Campbell puts it, where the self is conscious of *combating* his formed character (as is not infrequently the case), 'he surely cannot possibly suppose that the act, although his own act, *issues from* his formed character? I submit, therefore, that the self knows very well indeed – from the inner standpoint–what is meant by an act which is the *self's* act and which

nevertheless does not follow from the self's *character*. . . .[1]
The misguided, and as a rule quite uncritical, belittlement of
the evidence offered by inner experience has, I am convinced, been responsible for more bad argument by the
opponents of Free Will than has any other single factor. . . .
From phenomenological analysis of the situation of moral
temptation we find that the self as engaged in this situation is
inescapably convinced that it possesses a freedom of precisely
the specified kind, located in the decision to exert or withhold
the moral effort needed to rise to duty where the pressure of
its desiring nature is felt to urge it in a contrary direction. . . .
The creative act of moral decision is inevitably meaningless
to the mere external observer; but from the inner standpoint
it is as real, and as significant, as anything in human experience.'[2] So this brings us back to the concept of a two-way
relationship: this time between the character which largely
determines our choices and behaviour and the choices and
behaviour which, in their turn, play their part in forming our
character.

When we think of more trivial matters, I find it impossible
to agree with those who would assert that I have not got a
genuine power of choice, within certain limits, as to whether I
lay down my pen at this point or write another sentence;
whether I choose this word or that – and, on re-reading what I
have written, insert or subtract a comma; whether I decide to
raise my arm or prefer to leave it where it is. There may often
be obvious reasons for my choice, or motives of which I am
myself unconscious; but it would need a cogency of argument
which I have never yet met to persuade me that no choice
whatever was genuinely open to me between each of these
apparent options, or that I have never enjoyed any freedom

---

[1] *Cf.* in this context Rom. 7:15–17 and 6:14–23. These passages teach that
the 'freedom' so many claim today is in fact bondage to self. The only real
possibility of freedom from self and sin can be found in 'bondage' to Christ,
which, paradoxically enough, sets a man truly free. Augustine's discussion
of *non posse non peccare* and *non posse peccare* (which would represent pure
determinism), and *posse peccare* and *posse non peccare* (which necessarily imply
a certain freedom of moral choice), is also relevant.

[2] C. A. Campbell, *Selfhood and Godhood* (George Allen and Unwin, London,
1957), pp. 177–179.

of choice whatever in any such decision. If I could believe that, then I could, I think, believe anything.

It is in fact exceedingly difficult to deny that anyone who is not mentally deficient has, within certain more or less definite limits, the power of choice between a given number of alternatives, and the subsequent ability to say meaningfully that he *could* have chosen or acted differently. This has on occasion been supported by the argument that, sometimes at least, 'on reflection and subsequent awareness of the consequences of a choice, all of us, when a similar set of alternatives is presented to us a second or third time, choose differently because we have been dissatisfied with the consequences of the former choice'.[1] But this is not, of course, to exclude causality; on the contrary, it is to assert that 'causality itself is a primary condition of meaningful choice'. Thus H. W. Hintz argues that to deny this must imply not only a doctrine of fatalism but almost total irrationality in human experience. Rather, I would myself commend the view he attributes to John Dewey that 'each man is *responsible* for making the best choice available to him *within* the scope of his limitations and his powers'.[2]

To minimize or seek to discount moral responsibility is, in reality, to debase the essential dignity of man. This seems to me to represent a very dangerous tendency in much psychiatric treatment. Almost every fault or failing is blamed on the patient's circumstances or on someone else: the mother who failed to give him her breast, the father who was not sufficiently appreciative, the mistakes which others made in his early training, or the deficiencies in the society in which he grew up. No doubt many of these alleged shortcomings in other people, or in society itself, are true enough, and have indeed given rise to temperamental or other handicaps which the patient will have to face and overcome. But the fact remains, I believe, that the great majority of these handicaps *can* be overcome, and that the very effort involved in doing this may temper the character as fire tempers steel. This has been demonstrated in practice by O. Hobart Mowrer, and his school of psychiatry, in the United States. Although himself working on strictly humanistic principles, he passionately

[1] *Determinism and Freedom*, p. 164.   [2] *Ibid.*

believes in facing a patient's problems fairly and squarely,
getting him to see and acknowledge where he has himself
gone wrong or is now failing to rise to his moral responsibilities,
and showing him how he can put this right. This method of
treatment seems to have produced dramatic results not only
among 'neurotic' but also 'psychotic' patients.[1]

We shall be concerned with the Christian view of determinism and freedom of moral choice a little later in this chapter.
But it is pertinent in this context to make the point that almost
everyone admits that we *could* have acted otherwise than we
did, in many different contexts, provided that some of the
conditions had been different – and, especially, if we had in
fact so *wished*. But, the argument often runs, the fact is that
we could not have wished otherwise than we did. This is a
bold assertion, quite incapable of proof, summed up by
Russell in the aphorism: 'We can do as we please but we
can't please as we please.' But it is a common phenomenon in
the Christian life for the sincere Christian to tell his Lord that
he is not, in fact, willing to take a specified course of action,
or even for some particular change to be effected in his circumstances or way of thought, but that he is 'willing to be
made willing'.[2] And if it is objected that this is merely pushing
the problem one stage further back, and that we cannot of
ourselves even be willing to be made willing, I should give a
double reply: first, that each step further back one takes in
this sort of discussion, the more wildly doctrinaire the determinist argument must necessarily become; secondly, that this
is in fact an experience to which many Christians can give
testimony – and to which the only intelligent answer from the
non-Christian is that, should someone really believe in God and
fundamentally wish to do his will, then all the rest is perfectly
intelligible.

[1] *Cf.* Jay E. Adams, *Competent to Counsel* (Presbyterian and Reformed
Publishing Company, 1970), pp. xvi and *passim;* O. Hobart Mowrer, *The
Crisis in Psychiatry and Religion* (Van Nostrand Company, Princeton, 1961).
[2] *Cf.* Phil. 2:12 and 13. Way's paraphrase runs: 'Work out, with fear and
self-distrust, your own salvation. You have not to do it in your unaided
strength: it is God who is all the while supplying the impulse, giving you the
power to resolve, the strength to perform, the execution of his good
pleasure.' Arthur S. Way, *Letters of St Paul and Hebrews* (Macmillan, London,
1926), p. 156.

THE PHILOSOPHICAL APPROACH

We have already, and inevitably, strayed at times from physiology and psychology into what might more appropriately be regarded as a philosophical approach to this problem. But here the major debate turns on the exact content given to the word 'determinism'. Thus it is easy enough to concede that almost everything that happens has been 'caused' by some previous event or condition (although it is true, of course, that this statement would be strongly challenged by many physicists, and that it can never be accepted as in any sense axiomatic). But the basic problem is not so much the existence of causation as the interaction of different chains of causation.

A rock suddenly hurtles down a mountain, for example, and rolls straight in front of a car which is negotiating a narrow road. This prompts the driver to swerve, and he injures a doctor travelling in the opposite direction on a bicycle. As a result the doctor is delayed in reaching a scientist who urgently needs medical help, his prescription reaches a chemist just after he has closed his shop and gone away on a social call, and the scientist dies without having committed to paper a major scientific breakthrough to which his research has just pointed the way.

Now it is easy enough to trace a chain of causation in this whole sequence of events. Each item has unmistakably been caused by another. It might equally be possible, moreover, to discern a convincing chain of causation in each of the component parts. Thus there is, no doubt, a sound explanation why that particular piece of rock broke off from the side of a cliff, and started its descent, at that particular time. Similarly, there was probably a good reason why the motorist was winding his way along that particular road; and there may well have been an adequate explanation of the speed at which he was travelling, the degree of concentration he was devoting to his circumstances, and the way in which he reacted to the descent of the piece of rock. The doctor's journey in the opposite direction was, let us assume, directly attributable to a telephone call from the sick scientist's wife; and there may have been cogent reasons why the chemist shut his shop somewhat earlier than usual. There may even be some very adequate explanation why the scientist had the flash of intuition which led to his breakthrough and why he had not yet communicated this discovery to anyone else. As for his death, this may well have been the direct result of the delay in obtaining the requisite drugs. None of these chains of causation causes me the slightest difficulty.

It is when we begin to put them all together that the difficulty begins. Why, we wonder, did the fall of the rock coincide with the approach of the car from one direction and that of the doctor from the other? Was the whole sequence 'inevitable', not merely in the sense that one thing led to another but in the sense that there was some reason not apparent to the human mind why so many contingent events were so interwoven as to lead to the tragic result that a major scientific discovery was lost to man?

Much the same question could, of course, be posed in simpler terms. A mathematician, let us suppose, has been pondering some abstruse problem for years, but has made little or no progress. Then, one afternoon, he goes out to buy some toothpaste, he just misses a bus, he walks to the next bus stop, and in so doing he chances to read an advertisement about mowing machines. So he looks in at a shop to make enquiries about a new mower, and in the course of conversation the salesman makes a seemingly irrelevant remark which starts the mathematician off, in a way very difficult to account for, on a train of thought which leads to the flash of intuition which reveals the secret which he has been seeking so long. Here most of the chain of causation is, again, obvious enough; but can we really accept the idea that the whole sequence of events – the need for toothpaste, the timing of the bus, the advertisement, the conversation, the remark, the train of thought, and the flash of understanding – was either 'predictable' or 'foreordained' by some blind destiny? This was, it seems, Voltaire's view when he wrote: 'Everything happens through immutable laws... everything is necessary...' "There are", some persons say, "some events which are necessary and others which are not." It would be very comic that one part of the world were arranged, and the other were not; that one part of what happens had to happen and that another part of what happens did not have to happen. If one looks closely at it, one sees that the doctrine contrary to that of destiny is absurd . . .'[1]

It is noteworthy, in this context, that C. S. Lewis insists that 'What the Naturalist believes is that the ultimate Fact, the thing you can't go behind, is a vast process in space and time which is *going on of its own accord*. Inside that total system every particular event (such as your sitting reading this book) happens because some other event has happened; in the long run, because the Total Event is happening. Each particular thing (such as this page) is what it is because other things are what they are; and so, eventually, because the whole system is what it is. All the things and events are so completely inter-locked that no one of them can claim the slightest indepen-dence from "the whole show" . . . Thus no thoroughgoing Naturalist believes in free will: for free will would mean that human beings have the power of independent action, the power of doing something more or other than what was involved by the total series of events. And any such separate power of originating events is what the Naturalist denies. Spontaneity, originality, action "on its own", is a privilege reserved for "the whole show", which he calls Nature.'[2] But this, as we have seen, leaves no real place for logical thought. And it is significant that all arguments about the validity of thought, as Lewis points out, make a tacit exception in favour of the thought which happens, at that moment, to be in the mind of the one who puts forward the argument. 'The Freudian and the Marxist attack traditional morality precisely on this ground – and with wide success. All men accept the principle.'[3] So, he argues, 'rational thought is not simply and solely part of the system of nature. Within each man there must be an area (however small) of activity which is – in some sense – outside or independent of her.'[4] It would, no doubt, be closer to contemporary thought to express Lewis's point about free-

---

[1] *Cf.* Paul Edwards, in *Determinism and Freedom*, edited by Sidney Hook, p. 108.   [2] C. S. Lewis, *Miracles*, pp. 10 f.
[3] *Ibid.*, p. 39.   [4] *Ibid.*, p. 31.

will, spontaneity and action 'on its own' in terms of that 'number of possible programmes of action of equal potential or valency' (having regard to the stimuli to which a man is subject at the time) between which he has the possibility of making a choice which cannot confidently be prognosticated in terms which go beyond theories of probability.[1] But this leaves Lewis's basic argument unimpaired.

Put in other terms, it may be said that, while man is part of nature, he is not – as F. R. Barry argues – 'contained in nature. He stands, as it were, outside it and looks at nature, just as, in the mystery that we call self-consciousness, mind stands "outside" itself and looks at itself, and the self passes judgement on the self ("You know that you need not have done that; you ought to be ashamed of yourself"). If he were no more than a part of nature he could not be consciously aware of nature nor ask the question how he is related to it. . . . The divide, as I have said, seems to run within ourselves. There is unsolved mystery within ourselves. We are in the world, but in some way or other outside the world. . . . We speak about moral obligation, that is, about something other than ourselves and maybe in conflict with our inclinations, which we recognise as having a *claim* upon us. It speaks to us, as it were, from outside ourselves.'[2]

This brings us, I suppose, to the distinction between what has sometimes been called 'soft' and 'hard' determinism. If we opt for 'soft' determinism, in the sense in which I would wish to use that term, we come back, as it seems to me, to the two-way relationship to which we have already referred, under the headings of both physics and psychology. There may often, no doubt, be a clear-cut sequence of events, without which some eventual situation could never have been reached. But at each stage at which a sentient human being intervenes there is a relative, rather than finally and inexorably objective, quotient – a factor which may well be described as 'caused' but which need not necessarily have been 'inevitable'. In other words, it is perfectly possible – according to this

---

[1] See pp. 19f. above. But *should* it ever be possible to go beyond theories of probability, MacKay's reasoning would still be valid.
[2] F. R. Barry, *Secular and Supernatural* (SCM Press, London, 1969), p. 134.

view of the doctrine of determinism – to postulate that actions are 'causally determined', on the one hand, but that the agent *could* have acted differently, on the other. If, on the other hand, we opt for 'hard' determinism, in the sense which necessarily implies a 'closed' universe in which every physical happening, every thought of the human mind, every choice of the human will, and all the complex inter-relationships of different individuals with each other and with the circumstances which impinge upon them, all work according to some inexorable decree, then I must ask one question and make one assertion.

The question is this: what was it, then, which first began this whole chain of events, which settled this inexorable decree? If we could trace everything far enough back, would we eventually reach the one and only example of pure 'chance'? If so, is the whole universe, in the final analysis, meaningless and utterly inscrutable? This is, of course, a very common attitude today, especially among existentialists. They are comparatively united in asserting that we live in an absurd, ridiculous, meaningless universe in which there is nothing valid except self-authentication – whether through an act of the will, as a writer like Albert Camus would maintain, or through a vague feeling of dread, as Martin Heidegger would affirm.[1] Most of our contemporary humanists, however, would – I think – assert their faith in some more or less logical process of evolution. But must there not have been some 'uncaused cause' which started this process off; some plan, however little we can discern it, behind it all?

And the assertion flows directly from the question: that to believe in a totally 'closed' universe, in which every detail corresponds with some inexorable decree, seems not only to fly in the face of part of the available evidence, but to demand the most gigantic act of blind faith. The evidence to which I refer is the distinction, emphasized by C. S. Lewis, between what he somewhat naively[2] terms 'reason' and 'nature' –

[1] *Cf.* Francis Schaeffer, *The God who is There* (Hodder and Stoughton, London, 1968), p. 24.

[2] I say 'naively' because there is a very real sense, of course, in which 'reason' is in fact part of 'nature'. The distinction Lewis intends is between the initiative a man may take, based on reason and experience, to intervene in, and even manipulate, what may be termed the 'natural course of things'.

although I should myself differ from Lewis when he says that, at the frontier between the two, we find only 'one-way traffic'. He is clearly correct when he says that rational thought can 'induce and enable us to alter the course of Nature – of physical nature when we use mathematics to build bridges, or of psychological nature when we apply arguments to alter our emotions'.[1] Had he been alive today he might well have found a still more cogent example in the ability of doctors to 'play God', even now, by constructing what Ritchie-Calder terms a 'human artifact' as a result of surgical plumbing or, perhaps, by artificially mating two geniuses separated from each other by generations – or, in future, by feats of genetic manipulation with even more incalculable possibilities. But can it be postulated that all this is predetermined, or the inevitable outcome of irresistible impulses? On the contrary, as Desmond Pond has argued, one of the essential points which would seem to distinguish human beings from their nearest biological neighbours, monkeys, is 'the capacity to have served up, in the central part of the brain, vast numbers of possible courses of action'; and it is obvious that today man is able continually to *extend* this ever-widening sphere in which he has the possibility – indeed, the imperative duty – of making responsible moral choices. Where Lewis goes wrong, as I see it, is in not perceiving that, far from finding only 'one-way traffic', we continually discover a two-way relationship. As for the act of faith, this belief in a minutely ordered universe in which every detail works according to a pre-ordained plan, could (in my view) make sense *only* in theological terms – and, indeed, in terms of a very extreme form of theology. So it is to the theological approach to this subject that we must now turn.

THE THEOLOGICAL APPROACH

The most extreme example of theological determinism of which I have any knowledge is the doctrine of the strictest – and, indeed, the most influential – school of Islamic orthodoxy, the Ash'ariyya. A man hears the buzzing of a fly, so he stretches out his arm, picks up a fly-swat, waits until the fly

[1] C. S. Lewis, *Miracles*, p. 29.

alights on his leg, strikes at it and kills it. Or so it appears to
him. In reality, however, the whole operation derives directly
from the creative power of God. It is he who creates and recreates the atoms which make up the man's ear and his hear-
ing, the fly and the buzzing sound it seems to make, the fly-
swat and the man's leg – each, instant by instant, in the
different positions they assume. And it is also he who creates
and recreates the cells which comprise the man's brain, and
who effects in them those chemical changes which make it
appear to him that it was the buzzing of the fly which prompted him to stretch out his arm for the fly-swat, his experience
of similar incidents in the past which suggested to him that he
should wait until the fly settled, and his own decision which
precipitated the fatal blow. This impression of independent
choice and action is explained by al-Ash'arī by the postulate
that God creates in man the power to choose, and he then
'creates in him the action corresponding to the power and
choice thus created'. So the man's action is in fact created by
God in both its initiative and production; but it is, in al-Ash'-
arī's phrase, *acquired* by the man (who is himself, of course,
being continually created and recreated by God). 'By acquisi-
tion (*kasb*) is meant' – to quote D. B. Macdonald – 'that it
corresponds to the creature's power and choice, previously
created in him, without his having the slightest effect on the
action. He was only the *locus* or subject of the action.'[1]

It was in this way that al-Ash'arī tried to account for man's
apparent power of choice and moral responsibility. In reality,
however, it is clear that, according to this doctrine, it is God
who is the sole author of both good and evil. The Mu'tazilī
heresy had taught that God always acts in accordance with
justice; but al-Ash'arī would have none of this. To him God
was not only the creator of every atom in the universe
but the sole arbiter of exactly how it behaves moment by
moment – whether that atom was part of inanimate nature
or part of the mind, will or emotions of man. There were no
second causes; no other angle from which things could, with
any validity, be viewed; nothing whatever which God in any

---

[1] D. B. Macdonald, *Muslim Theology, Jurisprudence and Constitutional Theory*
(Charles Scribner's Sons, New York, 1903), p. 192.

B

sense desired which was not instantly accomplished, and nothing whatever which he deprecated which could ever come to be.

It is small wonder that Muslim thinkers have been confused, and deeply divided, on this most perplexing problem. Precisely the same has been true of Christian theologians. Any thinking man who believes both in a sovereign God and in the moral responsibility of man is face to face with the same basic enigma. If he puts an exclusive emphasis on the sovereignty of God he is left with men and women who are mere automata, who are moved about by the Almighty like pawns on a chessboard, and whose thoughts, choices, decisions and affections are all directly attributable to their sovereign Lord. But it is virtually impossible, on such premises, to attribute to them any moral responsibility whatever. But if, on the other hand, he gives an exaggerated emphasis to man's moral responsibility he is left with a God who is not really sovereign, for the accomplishment of his purposes is dependent on the will and choice of his creatures. It is crystal clear, moreover, that the Bible goes to neither of these extremes. On the contrary, it continually emphasizes both the sovereignty of God and the moral responsibility of men and women, and completely ignores the apparent anomaly this involves. It was thus that Peter, in his sermon on the day of Pentecost, stated unequivocally that 'this Jesus, delivered up according to the definite plan and foreknowledge of God, you crucified and killed by the hands of lawless men'.[1]

It seems clear, then, that there is a palpable difference between the relationship of God to inanimate nature, on the one hand, and his relationship to sentient creatures – and, pre-eminently, to man created in his own 'image and likeness' – on the other. In the first case there is no two-way relationship whatever, while in the second there is. In both cases, no doubt, the initiative is always with God; but in regard to inanimate objects there can, clearly, be no question of a response, while in regard to man there is, and must be, a human response to the divine initiative. It is thus that the Bible can and does, on occasion, speak of human beings, un-

[1] Acts 2:23.

like inanimate nature, as *resisting* the will of God, for God is not infrequently depicted as pleading with his creatures, and even pleading in vain. He is unquestionably sovereign, for he is all the time 'upholding the universe by his word of power';[1] but he has given human beings a degree of free will which is part of the very nature of man as man. So the Bible seems to set the absolute sense in which inanimate nature obeys the will of its Creator over against what may be termed the *permissive* will of God in allowing human beings to choose sin and to go their own way,[2] for we read that he does not *wish* that any should perish, but rather that 'all should reach repentance'[3], and that he 'desires all men to be saved and to come to the knowledge of the truth'.[4] But it is clear that there are many who do not repent and who do not come to the knowledge of the truth.

The Bible is emphatic, again, that God is omniscient, and that he knows all things from the beginning. If, then, he already knows the moral decisions I shall take next week, can I really be said to be in a position to exercise any genuine moral choice? This brings us back to the problem posed by D. M. MacKay in relation to his imaginary 'Super-scientist', who might in theory be able to read the cells of a man's brain – and the whole inter-acting universe – in such a way as to predict his future actions. But MacKay argued[5] that there could be no such prognostication of a future decision which would have any claim to the unconditional acceptance of the person concerned, for it was demonstrably true that, at the time concerned, he had not yet in fact made up his mind; and if the Super-scientist's prediction were in any way made known to him, then the chemical composition of his brain cells would be instantly changed, and the whole problem made devoid of meaning. And he also argued that the same would be true of anyone in dialogue, or any kind of reciprocal relationship, with the man who had not yet made up his mind. It would only be a 'Super-scientist' who could read a man's brain without any sort of contact or relationship with him

---

[1] Heb. 1:3.
[2] *Cf.* Rom. 1:24, 26, 28.   [3] 2 Pet. 3:9.   [4] 1 Tim. 2:4.
[5] D. M. MacKay, *Freedom of Action in a Mechanistic Universe*, pp. 29 ff.

whatever who could, even on the most extreme mechanistic theory, predict his future decisions and choices with any certainty.

In one respect, as MacKay suggests, there is a parallel here with the theological problem of divine sovereignty and human responsibility, although he rightly insists that the enigma must remain beyond the comprehension of our finite minds. There is a very real sense in which God is outside the space–time continuum in which we, his creatures, live. For him there is no past, present or future, but all is one eternal present. So another way of saying that God knows and can predict our future choices and actions would be to say that he here and now sees us choosing and acting in a way which, from our point of view, is still future. Yet there is another sense in which God is inside the space–time continuum in which we live, for he is immanent as well as transcendent, and he remains in dialogue, and in a living relationship, with us his creatures. It is in this way, therefore, that the two-way relationship to which we always seem to come back may be said to exist between God and man – for in man, as distinct from inanimate nature, there is a genuine moral responsibility, together with the capacity (indeed, the necessity) for a voluntary response to the divine initiative.

Much the same theological approach would seem to apply to our psychological make-up, whether this is the result of heredity or the experiences of early childhood. We have seen that we all find ourselves pre-conditioned in certain ways, with instincts and reactions we can only dimly understand and can only in part control. Nor do we live, in any valid sense, in a 'closed' universe. On the contrary, the universe is open to spiritual powers, both good and evil, and man is by no means the splendidly independent creature he sometimes imagines himself to be. The Bible clearly teaches that it is Satan who blinds men's minds to the truth about God and about themselves, and that it is God who 'shines in our hearts' to give us a knowledge of the truth in Christ. But the Bible also asserts that, once quickened to new life, we are not by any means slaves to desires and choices over which, as some would have us believe, we have no control whatever. We may not be able to produce in ourselves right desires, right conduct, or good characters; but there is a very real sense in which the choice is ours whether we hand ourselves over to God, who can and does little by little transform our desires and reform our conduct, or to Satan, who works in us in precisely the opposite way.[1] It has, indeed, been demonstrated that the type of therapy advocated by O. H. Mowrer[2] can be used effectively, even among those classified as mentally ill, by a Christian who puts a primary emphasis on an acknowledgement of personal sin, an assurance of forgiveness through Christ's atoning death, and an appropriation of his supernatural grace for the future.

It seems clear, moreover, that it is only as responsible moral beings that we could ever be called 'sons' of God. The Creator God can fashion the minutiae of electrons which no microscope can detect, the limitless spaces of the universe which no telescope can reveal, and the infinite varieties of colour and form in which he so obviously delights, without the need for any sort of response. But this would be meaningless in regard to sentient beings on whom he not only bestows his love but from whom, incredible though it may be, he desires love in return – for this would be valueless unless it comprised a voluntary element. Our love is poor and fitful, and never more than responsive, yet it means much to the one who is not only Creator but Father. No wonder, then, that the writer of the first Epistle of John exclaims: 'How great is the love that the Father has shown to us! We are called children of God! Not only called, we really are his children . . . Here and now, dear friends, we are God's children; what we shall be has not yet been disclosed, but we know that when he appears we shall be like him, because we shall see him as he is.'[3]

In C. S. Lewis's pungent words, the purpose of the powers of evil is diametrically opposite, at this point, to the purpose of their 'Enemy', God. 'To us', Screwtape says, 'a human is primarily food; our aim is the absorption of its will into ours, the increase of our own area of selfhood at its expense. But the obedience which the Enemy demands of men is quite a dif-

---

[1] Rom. 6:16—together with 2 Cor. 3:18 and 4:4, 6.
[2] See pp. 25f. above.   [3] 1 Jn. 3:1 and 2, NEB margin.

ferent thing. One must face the fact that all the talk about his love for men, and his service being perfect freedom, is not (as one would gladly believe) mere propaganda, but an appalling truth. He really *does* want to fill the universe with a lot of loathsome little replicas of himself – creatures whose life, on its miniature scale, will be qualitatively like his own, not because he has absorbed them but because their wills freely conform to his. We want cattle who can finally become food; he wants servants who can finally become sons.'[1] This is not poetic exaggeration, but sober (if almost unbelievable) fact, for we are specifically told that God's purpose is 'to bring many sons to glory'[2], all of whom would 'be conformed to the image of his Son'[3] and 'come to share in the very being of God'.[4]

CONCLUSION

But we must come back from these speculations – physical, psychological, philosophical and theological – to the everyday questions which will, for the most part at least, concern us in this book. Suffice it, then, to recognize the insoluble mystery which continually confronts us whenever we speculate about the extent to which individual human beings are preconditioned by the constitution and condition of their brains, by the psychological make-up they have inherited or acquired, by the blind and inevitable course of 'nature' or by the sovereignty of a Creator God, to behave in the way they do; but, at the same time, unequivocally to affirm that there is no reason whatever to suppose that ordinary men and women are mistaken in their firm conviction that they have, within limits, a genuine freedom of choice and action, and that this necessarily entails a corresponding measure of moral responsibility. It is this which provides the necessary presupposition for all that will follow in the rest of this book.

[1] C. S. Lewis, *The Screwtape Letters* (Fontana, London, 1955), p. 45.
[2] Heb. 2:10.   [3] Rom. 8:29.   [4] 2 Pet. 1:4, NEB.

2 MORALITY IN THE PERMISSIVE SOCIETY

People continually talk today about 'The Permissive Society', and seem to take it for granted that this is a just description of the society in which we live. No-one seems to know how, when or where the phrase first originated (as is also, I think, true of the 'Welfare State'); but the first essential in any rational approach to this subject must be to make up our minds what the phrase really means, and how far it does in fact characterize contemporary life.

In his book on *Christian Freedom in a Permissive Society*,[1] John Robinson, formerly Bishop of Woolwich, has defined 'permissiveness', both for those who like it and those who dislike it, as suggesting 'freedom from interference or control, doing your own thing, love, laxity, licence, promiscuity – and, in terms of verbs, swinging, sliding, eroding, condoning'. This means, presumably, freedom from interference or control not only by the sanctions of the criminal law but by authority of any sort whatever – parental, civil or divine – or even from the constraints, such as they may be, imposed by public opinion. Put in other words, and rather more moderately, this represents the claim that individuals not only have the responsibility for making their own moral decisions, but the *right* to make them without any interference on the part of others; and that, if they themselves accept the implications of what they are doing, then what they do is for them morally justified – 'which means', as J. W. Bowker remarks, that 'the permissive society would be an endorsement of Mrs. Camp-

[1] J. A. T. Robinson, *Christian Freedom in a Permissive Society* (SCM Press, London, 1970).

bell's famous phrase, that people may do what they like as long as they don't do it in the streets and frighten the horses'.[1] But in this technological age, even this very limited restriction on freedom of personal behaviour is becoming increasingly irrelevant.

IS OUR SOCIETY PERMISSIVE?

Now is permissiveness in this sense characteristic of the society in which we live? As so often, the answer, I think, must be both 'yes' and 'no' at the same time. It is easy enough to think of certain aspects of life in which permissiveness, in this sense, seems to have run riot; and to these we must presently return. But let us recognize at once, and without equivocation, that there are other spheres of life in which the attitude of large sections of the community, and especially of the young, is much less 'permissive' today than was the case in former generations. Some forty years ago when I was myself a student, for example, we took the stark inequalities of society in a singularly permissive spirit. We even sang

> 'The rich man in his castle,
> The poor man at his gate,
> God made them high and lowly
> And ordered their estate'

without any real sense of incongruity. Domestic servants lived in frigid attics or dingy basements on a mere pittance; medical care was available to the poor only on the quite inadequate basis of the 'panel patient' system; and the inferiority of the coloured races was accepted as almost axiomatic. Private property, however disproportionately distributed, was regarded as sacrosanct, and the penalties of the criminal law were weighted much more heavily – in general terms – against infringements of rights of property than offences against the person.

Today, thank God, much of this has changed, and there is a very vocal demand that the many and grievous survivals of past evils and inequalities should be swept away. The Welfare

---

[1] 'The Morality of Personal Relationships', in *Making Moral Decisions*, edited by D. M. MacKinnon (SPCK, London, 1969), pp. 47 f.

State has remedied some of the more obvious forms of social injustice, although a vast amount still remains to be done. The Race Relations Acts, and other attempts to influence public opinion, are beginning to make a dent in the ugly phenomenon of racial discrimination in this country. And demonstrations of all sorts at least provide evidence of the detestation with which most of the younger generation regard the iniquities of apartheid in South Africa or Rhodesia, or the horrors of modern warfare in Vietnam.

But the fact remains that there is a strange inconsistency in the attitude of considerable sections of our community. The oppression and persecution of coloured people in South Africa is rightly condemned, but singularly few voices are raised to denounce the inhumanity of the treatment accorded to Baptists in Russia. There is a widespread and praiseworthy demand for freedom of speech – however forcible – in regard to views which accord with those of the sections of the community which make these demands, but a lamentable disregard for the rights of others to express their views with equal freedom. In other words, the 'permissive' society can be singularly intolerant to opinions which it deprecates. Often enough, it is only permissive in regard to the values which the individuals or groups concerned themselves embrace, and seeks to eliminate contrary views not by persuasion but by suppression.

The vagaries to which our society is prone can be seen in relation to one of the most controversial of contemporary issues: freedom of sexual expression. It is often regarded as almost axiomatic that an artist must be free to portray life exactly as he sees it, so nudity and sexual titillation on the stage are widely defended (for is not the human body a beautiful thing, and the sexual urge a God-given instinct?); and this freedom is even extended to the portrayal, in great detail, of sexual depravity and sadism, as providing a realistic picture of human life in the raw.

The ambivalence of this attitude can be seen if we ask ourselves whether an artist should be free to depict a member of one of the coloured races exploiting, in some repulsive way, his seemingly amiable and inoffensive white neighbours. This would, I think, be roundly – and rightly – condemned by the very persons who claim that, in matters of sex, the artist must be completely uninhibited. But why should the derisive or derogatory portrayal of a coloured person on the stage or screen be prevented – whether by public opinion or by the law? Presumably for one of two perfectly good reasons: either because it is intrinsically wrong (as many would allow), or because it is liable to have a damaging effect on the attitude or behaviour of some of those who view it. But if this last argument is accepted, then it can scarcely be denied that sadism, or sexual exhibitionism and titillation, can similarly affect some of those who view them. After all, if what we see and read has no effect whatever on our behaviour, then it is difficult to believe that so many millions of pounds would be spent on advertising, whether on television or in the press. So the problem can be reduced to the question of whether such portrayal is, or is not, intrinsically wrong, and whether an increase in behaviour of the nature concerned should, or should not, be encouraged in the community.

The thesis of those who regard themselves as 'progressive' in such questions is well known. They commonly argue that morality – and particularly sexual morality – is essentially a relative standard, which changes from age to age; that fornication, adultery and homosexual relations are condemned, no doubt, by those who believe in divinely-revealed principles of human conduct, but are on quite a different level for others – provided only that they involve no exploitation of the young or weak and do not constitute a public nuisance; and that the detailed portrayal of sex or sadism may well serve as an outlet which prevents, rather than stimulates, anti-social acts on the part of those who have an inclination towards such behaviour. As for the naked body or the sex act, should we not rid ourselves, once and for all, of any idea that they are other than beautiful?

But this largely misses the point. The sex act is certainly one of God's best gifts, and both pure and beautiful when it symbolizes and deepens the total commitment of two people to each other; but the symbolism – and even the act itself – becomes a travesty of this when it is simulated by actors or performed in public (which must, surely, tend to coarsen both those who portray it and those who watch its portrayal). A shapely body is one of the most beautiful things God ever made; but the spiritual quality of that beauty is destroyed if the circumstances of its display are vulgar or immodest. There is a reticence and seemly privacy which we ignore at our peril. As E. L. Mascall has put it: 'Living like a gorilla is a very good thing to do if you are a gorilla, and living like an angel is a very good thing to do if you are an angel. And neither of these tasks is very difficult for the being in question. If, however, you are a human being you can achieve true happiness only by living as a human being, and that is a much more difficult task.'[1] An animal can perform all its physical functions openly and innocently, but a human being is prostituting his very nature if he acts in the same way.[2] Most of us, moreover, find it hard enough to maintain a wholesome attitude to life without any unnecessary exposure to that which tends in the opposite direction. If fine and worthy literature and art have an influence for good – as, surely, few would deny – it seems only logical to conclude that cheap, tawdry and vulgar literature and art have a coarsening effect.

PORNOGRAPHY AND OBSCENITY

In this context people continually refer to developments in Denmark. It is frequently alleged that the recent abolition of the laws against pornography in that country has resulted in a 25% decrease in sexual crimes; and that the Danes themselves, once 'liberated', soon lost their interest in pornography, which then became primarily an attraction for those who live in less enlightened lands. But this is in fact a very dubious statement. No doubt there were some Danes, previously the victims of a prurient curiosity, who soon found their curiosity satiated and their sensibilities offended; but for others Malcolm Muggeridge's dictum that 'pornography is as habit-forming as benzedrine' is almost certainly true. A recent letter to *The New Statesman* by Joan Rockwell, of the Department of Sociology in the University of Reading,[3] states that whereas the

[1] E. L. Mascall, *The Importance of Being Human*, p. 33.
[2] *Cf.* a letter in *The Times* on 4 August 1970, by S. C. Woodward.
[3] July 1970.

incidence of minor sexual crime, such as indecency towards women and children, has markedly declined in Denmark, serious sexual crime, such as rape and crimes of violence, has hardly been affected at all. More significantly, the letter continues: 'An interesting and unexpected occurrence since the abolition of all restraints on pornography has been the *escalation* of porno, from books, photos and films to "live shows", now publicly advertised in the newspapers. I recently brought back from Denmark *Ekstra Bladet*, the afternoon tabloid. On two pages of classified ads there were 18 for different live-show clubs, offering such attractions as Topless or Nude Go-Go, Strip Tease, Masturbation ("Young, lovely girl"), Lesbian Intercourse, Copulation ("visible orgasm")' – and, believe it or not, even worse. So Miss Rockwell pungently asks whether all this constitutes the 'harmless and legitimate satisfaction of the requirements of deprived people (they sit at home leafing through their dirty books, or go to these shows, and this is socially preferable to having them inconvenience or commit criminal acts against others); or whether it is a gross exploitation of the performer, tending to degrade and debase the social idea of sexual relations based on personal relationships of affection or trust'.

Now it is no doubt true that 'live shows' have always been available for those who sought them out, and could pay the necessary prices; but they were certainly far less blatant, less advertised and less easily available than they are today. It is also true that few, if any, are compelled to attend such performances, or to indulge in pornography in any form. But the fact remains that commercial interests do their best to sell them, just as they do drugs; and if the weaker members of society may legitimately be protected, as far as this is possible, from the drug traffic, then why not from commercialized vice?

The very mention of 'protection', of course, inevitably raises the thorny question of how far legal sanctions may properly be used to preserve moral standards. This question is basic to any consideration of the permissive society from one point of view – for it has been pertinently remarked that the very word permissive suggests that 'there is a right inherent in society, or in the leading individuals in society, to exercise control' – and that they are failing in this duty, inasmuch as certain activities are 'permitted' which ought not to be 'permitted'.[1] I shall discuss this subject more fully in my next chapter, which will be concerned with 'Morality and the Law'; so in the present context I must confine myself to insisting that there is no inherent reason why the theatre, cinema and television should be treated on exactly the same footing as novels, poems or the press.

In a recent letter to *The Times*[2] this point has been made with his usual pungency and wit by A. P. Herbert, who can scarcely be regarded as a kill-joy obscurantist. He recalls that he himself once remarked that 'It is one thing for a novelist to describe John and Jane, an affianced couple, walking naked and beautiful across a secluded Cornish beach to the sea. It might be quite another thing to present this same on the stage'. He argues, moreover, that the Lord Chamberlain's much derided rule (in the days when he still exercised censorship over the theatre) that actresses might appear unclothed on the stage only on condition that they remained absolutely motionless was, in effect, an example of treating the 'Friends of Parity' (*i.e.* between the stage and other forms of art) on the basis of their own contentions. 'You say', he imagines the Lord Chamberlain as arguing, 'if a naked Venus in the Louvre or a public park does not offend, why should a naked Venus not be permitted on the stage? Well, if your naked Venus behaves like a statue in the park, there shall be no objection.[3] But if the statue in the park pranced about and made enticing movements she would not be allowed there – and I shall not allow such spurious statues on the stage.' But the law as it stands at present, A. P. Herbert continues, could scarcely be held to prohibit a sketch 'showing a number of men in the cells of a public lavatory (without the doors) doing veraciously what is ordinarily done there'. The activities portrayed would not be immoral or intrinsically undesirable; 'indeed, they are recommended by the medical profession'. But their portrayal

---

[1] *Cf.* Michael Keeling, *What is Right?* (SCM Press, London, 1969), p. 93.
[2] 26 August 1970.
[3] Although even so there is, it seems to me, a valid distinction between a real person and the reproduction of the human form in stone.

on the stage would be not so much obscene, in the technical definition of that term, as indecent and offensive. So he concludes by saying: 'My colleagues and I, in 1954, began a worthy struggle for reasonable liberty for honest writers. I am sorry to think that our efforts seem to have ended in a right to represent copulation, veraciously, on the public stage.'

It is, of course, stridently contended that it is utterly wrong to suggest that acts which would be deemed indecent if performed in a public park, whatever their intrinsic character in their proper setting, must be regarded as equally indecent if enacted on the stage or the screen. The distinction, it is argued, is obvious: that in a park we are concerned with the public at large, while in a theatre or cinema the audience presumably bought their tickets with some idea of what they were likely to see, and they were always at liberty to get up and go out. But the validity and relevance of this argument are open to serious question, particularly in the case of television. It is sometimes far from obvious what a programme will include, and it is often exceedingly difficult for an individual member of a family or social group to turn off the switch, go out of the room, or leave a party of friends at a theatre or cinema, whenever they feel a moral urge to do so. And evasive action of the last sort is available, in point of fact, even in a public park.

PATTERNS OF PERSONAL BEHAVIOUR

When we turn from the stage, screen or even printed page to patterns of personal behaviour, we are faced by a much more controversial phenomenon, for the extent to which sexual morality is really more permissive today than it was in the past is a matter of dispute. It seems reasonably clear that the 'upper classes' have almost always been somewhat lax; and little has in fact been known about the morality of the working classes. But there can be no doubt that the middle-class pattern of morality has undergone a marked change. In Victorian days middle-class men seldom married until they had made enough money to support a wife in much the same style as that in which she had lived in her father's house; young men very frequently satisfied their sexual appetites by associating with prostitutes; and there was an appalling exploitation of girls of very tender age. The morality of middle-class women, on the other hand, was rigidly protected; indeed, 'nice' women were scarcely credited with any sexual desires other than the fulfilment of their conjugal duties. Today all this has radically changed. Women are incomparably more free and their sexuality is accepted; the number of prostitutes has greatly diminished; and the equality of the sexes is commonly acclaimed. Much of this represents a gain, rather than a loss.

At the same time it seems clear that, among the middle classes at least, extra-marital sex is greatly on the increase; and it is indisputable, I think, that an uninhibited attitude to sexual experimentation is advocated as both natural and beneficial far more widely than in the past. Even among those who would deprecate promiscuity, moreover, many would condone sexual intimacy – heterosexual or even homosexual – provided only that it expresses what has been described as a 'tender, caring, responsible relationship'. We live in a society in which the prevalent ethos is that every conceivable desire should, so far as possible, be satisfied immediately. We want to keep up with the Joneses; to get a new car, house, furniture, washing machine or radio: so we get it at once, and hope to pay for it later. There is little wonder, then, that our children take the same attitude to sex.[1] A boy and girl feel an attraction for each other – or even something a good deal deeper; so they see no reason why they should not give the fullest expression to their affections and desires without restraint or delay. But the very insistence that sexual intimacy should always express a 'tender, caring, responsible relationship' – to which reference has been made above – should give them pause. Even if we leave on one side, for the present, any question of moral rules based on an objective or authoritative standard, a responsible human being must surely take account of the possible implications of his actions and behaviour, not only for his own psychological and spiritual development, but also that of the other party concerned? And many of those who act

[1] *Cf.* Douglas Rhymes, in *No New Morality* (Constable, London, 1964), pp. 46 f.

as confidants and advisers to students and young people have
testified to the psychological damage – and even the misery
and occasional tragedy – to which extra-marital sex not infrequently gives rise.

Again, reference is continally made to the enormous increase in the figures for divorce; and the conclusion is drawn
that the stability – let alone the sanctity – of marriage has been
gravely undermined. But we need to remember that the avail-
ability of divorce as a possible option is of very recent date –
except, that is, for the comparatively wealthy, and on very
narrowly defined grounds. Today people marry younger and
live to a greater age, so marriages are at risk over a far longer
period; the grounds for divorce have been widened; legal aid
has opened the divorce courts to all; and women have attained
much more economic independence. No wonder, then, that
the number of divorces has multiplied. But while, from one
point of view, this suggests a breakdown in both the stability
of marriage and the respect in which it is held, there is another
side to the picture. It can be argued that the real comparison
should be between the number of broken marriages, rather
than those dissolved by the courts, in different periods in our
history; or even that the desire to give a 'dead' marriage a
decent burial, and then to contract another – and hopefully a
more vital – legal union, rather than to continue in an illicit
relationship, represents a gain, rather than a loss, in the regard in which the whole institution of marriage is commonly
held. There is certainly substance in this argument; but there
are equally certainly elements in our contemporary society
which take a very light-hearted, or occasionally even hostile,
attitude to marriage.

Nor can we ignore the fact that personal moral decisions –
in every sphere of life – can never be wholly divorced from
considerations of the good of the community as a whole. It
was a realistic understanding of this fact which forced Sartre
to change his existentialist assertion that what is involved in
moral decision is exclusively personal – the progress of an
individual towards 'authentic living' (or living consistently,
and without pretence, in accordance with what he knows himself to be) – for his own brand of Marxism, in which he 'recog-

nised the reckless poverty' of the existentialist view, since the 'luxury of individual autocracy cannot be afforded while so many people throughout the world are in such desperate need', or while it 'ignores or treats with contempt the minimum right of other creatures to survive'. This is certainly an advance. And yet the existentialist and the Marxist views have 'the significant common ground' that there is no genuinely external moral standard to which the individual in existentialism, or the State in Marxism, has any obligation to conform.[1] In the one the only standard is self-authentication, and this might take the widest variety of different forms; and in the other every moral standard can – and should – be subordinated to the cause of 'revolution'. But this clearly leaves wide open both the nature of the revolution which is desirable or attainable, and the further question of whether the end can always justify the means.

But for the Christian other considerations also apply. To return for a moment to the question of sexual morality, the Bible tells us that 'everything that God created is good',[2] and certainly gives no countenance to any low view of the physical side of marriage (whatever some of the early Church Fathers may have believed). But the Bible also teaches that man is now a fallen creature, who finds it all too easy to turn *any* of God's gifts to the wrong use. This is no mere matter of theological dogmatism, but a realistic appraisal of human experience; for we all know well enough that we fall lamentably short even of our own ideals. To argue about a suitable code of morality for men and women who had never known sin, or the tension of moral temptation competing with their better instincts, is a profitless exercise. Even to talk, with John Robinson, of a scheme of ethics for 'man come of age' is in fact misleading, for man has not yet come of age and, left to himself, never will. To leave every decision to man's better judgment presupposes a moral perfection in human beings which contradicts the basic facts of life. This is precisely why the Bible includes (in both the Old and New Testaments) clearcut moral principles or 'laws' which represent the Maker's

[1] *Cf.* J. W. Bowker, in *Making Moral Decisions*, pp. 53 f.
[2] I Tim. 4:4, NEB.

instructions as to how the men and women he has made can
live the life he designed for them.

'SITUATION' ETHICS OR 'PRINCIPLED' ETHICS?

It is, of course, fashionable today, even in theological circles,
to pour scorn on the very idea of moral laws which 'come down
direct from heaven, and are eternally valid for human conduct',[1] while many people insist that morality should not be
regarded as consisting in obedience to law – whether that of
reason, nature, duty or God – but as behaviour directed to the
achievement of some specific purpose.[2] A striking illustration
of this attitude can be found in the very different stance towards sexual morality taken up by communism in different
parts of the world. In non-communist countries, communists
tend to support a very permissive attitude towards sex, and to
deprecate as reactionary all attempts to maintain, or to re-
instate, anything approaching traditional standards of morality. In countries in which communism has secured full control,
on the contrary, sexual freedom is by no means encouraged;
and Malcolm Muggeridge and others have commented that
sex is much less pervasive in Moscow, for example, than in
London or New York. This phenomenon can, I think, be
explained only on the basis that communists recognize, on
the one hand, that sexual laxity tends to undermine the
moral fibre of a democracy which they are seeking to destroy,
and that it is impossible, on the other, to achieve a high degree
of political and economic discipline unless there is a corresponding discipline in matters of sex. In other words, it would
scarcely be going too far to subscribe to the statement that the
morality of communism is 'wholly subordinated to the interests
of the proletarian class war'.[3]

Again, the section of society which we may loosely designate

[1] J. A. T. Robinson, *Honest to God* (SCM Press, London, 1963), p. 106.
[2] *Cf*. Douglas Rhymes, *No New Morality*, p. 8.
[3] *Cf*. the view of Øyrind Skard, President of the Norwegian National
Committee for Mental Health, in *Ideological Strategy* (Blandford Press,
London), pp. 65 f. – as quoted in Arnold Lunn and Garth Lean, *The New
Morality* (Blandford Press, London, 1964), pp. 38 f. *Cf*. also Douglas
Rhymes, *No New Morality*, p. 58.

as 'hippies' has revolted against conventional morality because they are totally out of sympathy with the contemporary
world. They are determined to stand for the importance of
the community or 'tribe' against an exaggerated individualism;
of aesthetic values against the utilitarianism of a technological
age; of the international brotherhood of man against a strident
nationalism; of pacifism against militarism; of a carefree detachment from everyday life against the soul-destroying mono-
tony of the rat-race; and of an uninhibited enjoyment of the
physical against what they regard as a false asceticism. And
even in much more conventional circles we find it increasingly argued that morality in the past was based on the con-
formity of behaviour to the standards set by the Christian
tradition, whereas today 'the moral duty of an individual
is seen to lie less in conforming to such generally accepted
standards than in realising his potentialities as an individual'.[1]
This attitude can be summed up in the clichés: 'People matter
more than codes' and 'Morals, like the Sabbath, were made
for man, not man for morals'.[2]

But while there is a very real sense in which both these last
statements are manifestly true, they can be used in a way
which is as specious and misleading as the false antithesis so
often made between law on the one hand and love on the
other – with the inevitable exaltation of the latter and derogation of the former. If this antithesis were true, then the choice
would indeed be obvious. But the idea that fallen man can
dispense with moral principles – except as mere 'guide-lines' –
and launch out on life with love as his only 'absolute', seems
to me absurd; for how can any of us be sure of knowing what
the highest love really demands, in all the complex relationships of life and its repercussions on other individuals and on
society – especially when we ourselves are under the influence
of strong emotional pressures? As B. H. Streeter justly remarks: 'When passion is the arbiter, my own case is always
recognised to be exceptional. . . . When Aphrodite whispers
in my ear, a principle which admits of no exception may nerve
me to resist; but if any exception is admitted, my case is cer-

---

[1] *No New Morality*, p. 20.
[2] *The New Morality*, p. 67.

tain to be one.'[1] To say with John Robinson that 'Love alone,
because, as it were, it has a built-in moral compass, enabling
it to "home" intuitively upon the deepest need of the other,
can allow itself to be directed completely by the situation. . . .
It is able to embrace an ethic of radical responsiveness, meet-
ing every situation on its own merits, with no prescriptive
laws'[2] is in practice wishful thinking. Far from God's laws
being set over against love, they are in fact designed to delineate
its proper manifestations and guard against its abuse – and
they can, in general, be shown to be both socially and psycho-
logically beneficial.

In any discussion of 'permissiveness' it is significant that one
of the basic New Testament definitions of sin is 'lawlessness'.
In society this represents anarchy; and in individual life a
freedom which would not really be freedom at all, for it would
in fact mean slavery to self rather than freedom from it. It is
also relevant that when St Paul discussed the 'signs' which
would herald the approaching end of the present age (which
is not by any means a popular subject today) he insisted that,
even in apostolic times, what he described as the 'mystery of
lawlessness' was already at work, but was kept in control;
whereas, when the present age drew to a close, this restraint
would be removed, and lawlessness would run riot.[3]

No wonder, then, that the Bible gives us moral 'laws' which
are much more than mere guide-lines; for they are principles
of abiding validity. It is true, of course, that in this very im-
perfect world two of these moral principles may sometimes
conflict; and then the only thing we can do is to try to choose
the lesser of two evils.[4] But that does not mean – as advocates
of 'Situational Ethics' would have us believe – that what we
then have to choose is intrinsically right and that the moral

---

[1] B. H. Streeter, *Adventure, the Faith of Science and the Science of Faith* (Macmillan, London, 1937), p. 125.
[2] J. A. T. Robinson, *Honest to God*, p. 115. But it is only fair to add that
John Robinson himself states that while this will, no doubt, be treated as a
licence to laxity, 'love's gate is strict and narrow and its requirements
infinitely deeper and more penetrating' (pp. 118 f.).
[3] *Cf.* 2 Thes. 2:3–10.
[4] This is not, of course, in any way to suggest that this is the only moral
problem we have to face.

principle which it breaks has no relevance or authority. It means that the act is contrary to a valid and authoritative principle, and must be deplored as such; but that, in all the circumstances of the particular case, this action must be regarded as less damaging than any alternative. Suppose, for example, one were standing on a lonely heath at a place where two footpaths diverged, and a small girl ran down one of them – only to be followed, three minutes later, by a man who had the appearance of a homicidal maniac and stopped to ask which way she had gone. No doubt the ideal course of action would be to calm him down, detain him, or otherwise deflect him from his apparent purpose; but, should all such efforts fail, one would surely have to say that the girl had gone in the opposite direction from that which she had in fact taken? This would involve telling a direct lie, which is in principle intrinsically wrong – and should always be recognized as such. But it would clearly be the lesser of two evils and therefore, in the circumstances, the right choice. Numerous examples, many of them much more complex and difficult, will occur to any thoughtful person – ranging, indeed, from questions of purely private morality to those which face a politician or nation (*e.g.* the use of whatever degree of force may be necessary to resist tyranny and injustice).[1]

William Barclay has suggested the analogy of dangerous drugs. There are, he insists, situations in which these may properly be prescribed by the most responsible doctor; but this does not mean that they are not intrinsically poison, or that they should not be labelled as such.[2] Fletcher's scorn about Cicero's assertion that 'only a madman could maintain that the distinction between the honourable and the dishonourable, between virtue and vice, is a matter of opinion, not of nature' is altogether misplaced; for, however much the adherents of Situation Ethics may deny this, certain actions *are* intrinsically virtuous or vicious as the case may be. It is conceivable, as Barclay observes, that Celtic might play Rangers or Arsenal Manchester United, in some distant Utopia, without either rules or a referee, but no-one in his

---

[1] *Cf.* pp. 84, 89, 95f., 101 below.
[2] William Barclay, *Ethics in a Permissive Society* (Fontana, London, 1971).

senses would suggest that anything other than chaos would
result if this were attempted today. Yet a wise referee will not
penalize an infraction of the rules which works out for the
benefit of the game as a whole rather than that of the one who
commits it; and the fact remains that, in the moral sphere, we
may on occasion be faced with what seems to be an inevitable
clash between two virtues, and the stark necessity, in the interests of all concerned, of sacrificing the one to the other.

But what, it may be asked, is the criterion by which we can
determine what is virtue and what is vice; what is the basis
and authority for any valid system of ethics? Even Fletcher
concedes that a responsible moral decision must be 'informed
by principles and guidance derived, not simply from your own
experience, but also from the collective experience of the
human race', while Robinson asserts that we must 'rely, in
deep humility, upon guiding rules, upon the cumulative
experience of one's own and other people's obedience. It is
this bank of experience which gives us our working rules of
"right" and "wrong", and without them we could not but
flounder'.[1] But Fletcher continually repeats that, while Situation Ethics is willing to make full and respectful use of principles, they must always be 'treated as maxims rather than
laws and precepts'[2]; and this provokes Bowker to the pertinent comment that 'it is precisely here that the weakness
of Situation Ethics appears: it is so preoccupied with saying
over and over again what status principles do *not* have – i.e.
they are not rules – that it gives far too little consideration to
the status they *do* have. We are told they are not rules, but
why then should we accept that they are guidance? Indeed,
how do we find out what they are? A "collective bank of
human experience" would contain, to put it mildly, a great
variety of material – would it not contain, for example, what
Hitler thought to be the most loving thing in his situation,
that genocide was ultimately beneficial to all concerned?'[3]

---

[1] J. Fletcher, *Situation Ethics* (SCM Press, London, 1966) and J. A. T.
Robinson, *Honest to God* (pp. 119 f.), as quoted by Bowker, in *Making Moral
Decisions.*
[2] *Situation Ethics*, p. 31.   [3] *Making Moral Decisions*, p. 58.

THE BASIS FOR MORAL PRINCIPLES

What, then, is our criterion? Are all moral statements, as has been widely argued, no more than expressions of opinion or exercises in value-judgment which are in no sense susceptible to proof? Can the judgments of each individual's conscience be dismissed as the accidental products of the cultural environment in which he happened to be born and brought up? This view, as R. Money-Kyrle points out, may seem to be supported by the wide variety of codes of social morality in different cultures which anthropologists have brought to light.[1] As a result the ethical relativist commonly renounces any claim to evaluate other people's moral standards, and is somewhat apologetic about his own. But is this attitude really tenable today, in the light of such phenomena as the Nazi attitude to the Jews, the communist attitude to individual liberty, or the South-African attitude to non-whites?[2]

Nor can any solution to the problem of ethics be found in theories of evolution, for there is in fact no logical connection whatever between moral standards and the evolutionary process.[3] It is fatally easy, moreover, to conclude that an 'absolute' standard is too stringent and exacting, and that it should, therefore, not only be abandoned in practice but also discredited in theory. So it is well to remember that 'hypocrisy begins not only when men fail to practise what they preach but also when they begin to preach what they practise. Victorian writers who went to bed with a mistress did not feel it necessary to persuade themselves and others that fornication was enlightened and adultery progressive.'[4] But what has been aptly described as 'fake-objectivity' of this sort is an ever present temptation, as Aldous Huxley confessed when he said:

---

[1] This has, however, often been greatly exaggerated. Almost all communities, for example, disapprove of murder, adultery or theft, although their definitions of what in fact constitute these offences may vary considerably.
[2] *Cf.* 'Psychoanalysis and Politics', as quoted in H. Guntrip, *Mental Pain and the Cure of Souls* (Independent Press, London, 1956), p. 176.
[3] *Cf.* Noel Annan, *Leslie Stephen* (MacGibbon and Kee, London, 1951), pp. 278, 214.
[4] Arnold Lunn and Garth Lean, *The New Morality*, p. 12.

'I had motives for not wanting the world to have a meaning;
consequently assumed that it had none, and was able without
any difficulty to find satisfying reasons for this assumption. . . .
The philosopher who finds no meaning in the world is not
concerned exclusively with a problem in pure metaphysics;
he is also concerned to prove that there is no valid reason why
he personally should not do as he wants to do, or why his
friends should not seize political power and govern in the
way that they find most advantageous to themselves. . . .
For myself, as, no doubt, for most of my contemporaries, the
philosophy of meaninglessness was essentially an instrument
of liberation. The liberation we desired was simultaneously
liberation from a certain political and economic system and
liberation from a certain system of morality. We objected to
the morality because it interfered with our sexual freedom;
we objected to the political and economic system because it
was unjust. The supporters of those systems claimed that in
some way they embodied the meaning (a Christian[1] meaning,
they insisted) of the world. There was one admirably simple
method of confuting these people and at the same time justi-
fying ourselves in our political and erotic revolt; we would
deny that the world had any meaning whatever.'[2]

The only answer to 'fake-objectivity' is to show that it is
false, either by reference to the motives which inspire it or to
an authoritative standard which it ignores or flaunts. So we
come back to the basic question whether, and where, such
an authoritative standard can be found. But if in fact there is a
God, and if he is interested in how his creatures live, would it
not stand to reason that he might be expected to have given
them some indication of the moral standards which accord,
not only with his own nature and character, but also with
theirs, as he intended them to be? He could have done this, of
course, in one (or both) of two ways: either by what has been
termed general revelation or natural law, on the one hand,
or by some special revelation – as in the Bible, for example –
on the other. That there is such a thing as general revelation

[1] But sometimes with *very* dubious authority.
[2] Aldous Huxley, *Ends and Means* (Chatto and Windus, London, 1937),
pp. 270–273.

the Bible itself asserts, for Paul insists that those who know no 'special' revelation 'display the effect of the law (*i.e.* God's law) inscribed on their hearts. Their conscience is called as witness, and their own thoughts argue the case on either side, against them or even for them'.[1] It will not do to discount the force of this passage – or, indeed, of any other reference to the law of God – by remarking that the doctrine that there is any 'absolute standard' is today honoured 'much more in the breach than the observance'.[2] This is no doubt true; but it was at least equally true in the days of the early church, when Paul wrote that men and women 'know well enough the just decree of God, that those who behave like this deserve to die, and yet they do it; not only so, they actually applaud such practices'.[3]

But why should we turn to the Bible as our source of authority in this question of moral standards? It is frequently argued that this is a very narrow-minded, and even untenable, attitude today, in the light of contemporary knowledge of other religions. Surely the Bible can no longer be accepted as providing any authoritative standard – except, at most, in terms of the morality which is still, in general terms, largely accepted in those parts of the world which follow the Judaeo-Christian tradition? As soon as we turn our eyes further afield, the position would seem to be very different; for has not the Muslim an equal right to regard the Qur'ān as enshrining an authoritative declaration of the divine will, and the Hindu to point to the way of life adumbrated in his sacred scriptures as equally binding? And, whatever view we may take of ethical relativism, what answer can we give to the logical positivist when he asserts that moral statements are essentially emotive rather than rational, that their objective validity cannot possibly be proved, and that they amount in reality to no more than a declaration of personal conviction that certain actions

[1] Rom. 2:15, NEB.
[2] *Cf.* J. A. T. Robinson, *Honest to God*, p. 109. But, again, it is only fair to add that John Robinson rests his main argument not on this point, but on the fact that what we may loosely term the 'old morality' represents, in his opinion, a serious distortion of 'the teaching of Jesus'.
[3] Rom. 1:32, NEB.

are desirable or undesirable – or, in the Christian view, commanded or forbidden by the Creator?

In this context it must be conceded that the 'proof' the Christian would adduce cannot, in the nature of the case, represent propositions which are necessarily self-authenticating. The Christian's contention – whether he is face to face with the logical positivist or the sincere adherent of some other religion – is based on the whole body of historical and experimental evidence[1] which has led him to the firm conclusion that Jesus Christ was not merely a supremely wise religious and moral teacher, but the incarnate Son of God – and that the moral teaching which he gave is therefore of unique authority. And he will also point to what are to him, at least, convincing reasons for believing that that teaching has come down to us in a reliable form; that it was, in part, authoritatively explained and applied by the apostles; and that Christ himself bore testimony to the validity of the moral teaching enshrined in the Old Testament. But the Christian will concede that biblical statements, however valid and authoritative in themselves, should not be taken in isolation and applied in a rigid and unimaginative way: they must be systematically considered in their proper context; must be interpreted in the light of their original import; and must then be applied – to the best of our ability – to the problems of today.

But however convinced Christians may be in their own minds, what possible right have they – it is often asked – to force their opinions on others? This question really covers two distinct points: first, whether God's moral laws are designed for believers only, or for man as man; and, secondly, to what extent they can, or should, be forced on the community at large. To the second point the obvious answer is that, in a democracy, a minority must of necessity seek to persuade rather than compel; and, even if he were in totally different circumstances, a Christian should always respect other people's liberty of conscience in the same way in which he demands this for himself. But surely he has the right to try to persuade his fellow-citizens by any means in his power – whether private

[1] I have examined this evidence in my book *Christianity: the witness of history* (Tyndale Press, London, 1969).

or public – of what he profoundly believes to be most beneficial for society? And this brings us back to the first point: that the principles or 'laws' of moral conduct revealed in the Bible are no sequence of arbitrary or meaningless rules, but rather what I have described as the 'Maker's instructions' as to how the creatures he has made can best live lives which are satisfying to themselves and beneficial to others.

Finally, it is relevant to note that in the teaching of Christ we find what J. W. Bowker describes as a combination of 'absolute demand in terms of what human beings at their best can achieve' – or God's own standard for human living – with 'unyielding compassion and help for those who have fallen short. It is a refusal to diminish the splendour and destiny of men in relation to God, and it is a refusal to regard as trivial their failures to achieve it. . . It was because the demand was of such extreme clarity that compassion, genuine engagement and sympathy, could arise from it; for the demand places a value on people, and on what their lives are worth, which cannot arise in any other way. These two, demand and compassion, which might so easily have existed in a hopeless and impossible tension, were held together in the word and in the activity of "forgiveness".'[1] So the Christian, while he can never live a life which is in any sense antinomian, and while he must always accept the law of Christ as demanding his whole-hearted obedience, will never regard himself as 'under the law' (in Paul's words) in so far as his hope and assurance of salvation are concerned, but rather – and emphatically – 'under grace'.[2] This fundamental fact will, in part, be the subject of my last chapter.

[1] J. W. Bowker, in *Making Moral Decisions*, pp. 69f.
[2] Rom. 6:14.

3 MORALITY AND LAW I
General considerations

In my last chapter we noted in passing that any reference to a 'permissive society' gives rise not only to the question of *what* is permitted, but also to that of *how* this is 'permitted' and what such permission entails. When we think of a society which is the reverse of permissive, for example, do we envisage a community of people who habitually impose upon themselves a strict code of ethical conduct and are intolerant of any failure in their own lives to conform to the standard they have set themselves; or do we think of a community with a communal code of morality which is imposed on an aberrant minority by a majority which is intolerant of any deviation? And if our concept of the role of society includes the propriety – or at least the inevitability – of such imposition, then how is this to be effected? Is it reasonable to believe that this can be done by the force of education, public opinion and social pressure alone, or must it not also in some cases involve the civil or criminal law – together with police, courts, litigation and sanctions?

On a practical level it is clear that no community of men and women has ever existed which has not felt the need for law enforcement in some shape or form. Individuals who permit themselves to behave in whatever way they feel inclined must inevitably, sooner or later, come into conflict with others who act with an equal lack of self-restraint – or, indeed, even with those who do not. Social life is impossible, therefore, without some definition of the 'rights' of individual members of the community and a recognition of the fact that the liberty of each must be restricted at least to the extent which is necessary to ensure that its exercise does not injure the rights or invade the liberties of others. And this, in its turn, involves the concept of law and order.

It is, of course, notorious that there is no facet of the law which has caused writers on jurisprudence more difficulty than the definition of what, precisely, they mean by the term 'law'. Nor is it only academic lawyers who find it difficult to distinguish between such concepts as law, morality, custom, obligation, *etc.*; for this same difficulty is inherent in the pattern of thought in a number of great world religions.

MORALITY AND LAW IN MUSLIM AND HINDU THOUGHT

In Islam, for example, the Sharī'a, or law of God, is absolutely fundamental; but it is noteworthy that this vast system of law has been aptly described as a 'scheme of duties' rather than a system of strictly legal precepts. It covers every possible aspect of human life – ritual and social, private and public, national and international – and it bases its propositions fairly and squarely on what Muslims believe to be divine revelation; for man is utterly incapable of himself (according to the strictest school of Muslim orthodoxy) of distinguishing between good and evil, virtue and vice. On this view, indeed, there is no such thing as virtue and vice in the abstract, for every human action derives its ethical quality solely from the fact that it has been commanded, recommended, left legally indifferent, reprehended or positively forbidden by the Almighty. God does not command the good because it is inherently good, or forbid the evil because it is intrinsically evil; on the contrary, the whole structure of morality rests exclusively on the arbitrary fiat of the divine will. In terms of the later debate between the Christian Schoolmen about the basis of morality, this means that the Ash'ariyya school of Muslim thought takes substantially the same line as Duns Scotus and William of Occam: for it is said of the former that he believed that 'morality depends on the will of God. A thing is good not because it corresponds to the nature of God or, analogically, to the nature of man, but because God so wills'; and of the latter that in his view 'the natural moral law is positive law, divine will. An action is not good because of its suitableness to the essential nature of man . . . but because God so wills. God's will could also have willed and decreed the precise opposite . . . Thus, too, sin no longer contains any intrinsic element of immorality . . . it is an external offence against the will of God.'[1]

Now it is true that the Ash'ariyya, although the dominant school of Islamic orthodoxy, was by no means unchallenged among Muslim thinkers. Other schools of thought were in far closer agreement with those Schoolmen who found the basis for natural law and morality in the mind of God rather than the will of God.[2] The Mu'tazila, in particular, insisted that the reason why God has commanded some things and forbidden others is that the first are intrinsically good and the second inherently evil, and that man can on occasion perceive the moral nature of certain behaviour even without the aid of divine revelation. Yet others, such as the Māturīdīs and many Ḥanafī jurists, took up an intermediate position. They agreed with the Mu'tazilīs that virtue and vice are qualities inherent in certain types of behaviour, and that man can in some cases perceive this of himself; but, unlike the Mu'tazilīs, they refused to admit that the perception of what is virtuous or vicious involves any apprehension of a divine command or prohibition,[3] or that there can be any moral responsibility to practise virtue or shun vice before the divine law has been promulgated. This corresponds with the almost certainly mistaken interpretation which is often put on Paul's statement that 'Sin indeed was in the world before the law was given, but sin is not counted where there is no law'[4] – for this verse is best understood, I think, as teaching that long before the Mosaic law was promulgated the law of con-

---

[1] H. A. Rommen, *The Natural Law*, translated by T. R. Hanley (Herder Book Co., London, 1947), pp. 58ff.

[2] It would seem clear that the Schoolmen were influenced by this conflict of view between Muslim theologians, but I do not know of any detailed study on this subject.

[3] *Cf.* in this context my paper on 'Reflections on Law – Natural, Divine and Positive', in the *Journal of the Victoria Institute*, 1965.

[4] Rom. 5:13, RSV.

science, at least, was in existence; for sin indubitably did exist, and there can be no sin where there is no law.[1]

But however this may be, it is clear that Muslim theologians, like the Christian Scholastics who were to follow them, regarded either the mind or will of God as the ultimate basis for both morality and law. And this, in its turn, means that there was little difference for them between morality and law – as is, indeed, immediately apparent to anyone who studies the Sharīʿa. First, it is significant that four of the five categories under which, as we have seen, human actions are frequently subsumed by Muslim lawyers are what is commanded, recommended, reprobated or forbidden by the Almighty; and it is only in regard to the intervening category, *i.e.* those things which are classified as legally indifferent by the divine law, that human legislation is, strictly speaking, permissible. Secondly, it is obvious, I think, that actions which are recommended but not positively commanded, on the one hand, and reprobated but not actually forbidden, on the other, can scarcely be justiciable before any human tribunal; and an examination of what is included in the categories of actions which are positively commanded or forbidden shows that the enforcement of many of these injunctions and prohibitions must of necessity be left to the judgment of the hereafter. It seems clear, then, that a distinction may legitimately be made between those parts of the Sharīʿa which could be the subject of human litigation and those which must be left to the verdict of public opinion or the bar of eternity – which is, of course, precisely the distinction commonly made by writers on jurisprudence between law and morality. And this conclusion is reinforced by the fact that, alongside this basic scale of values (*i.e.* what is commanded, recommended, reprobated, forbidden, *etc.*), references also occur in Islamic law to a more strictly 'legal' scale (*e.g.* contracts which are 'valid', 'irregular' or 'void'). Muslim jurists, moreover, commonly take the view that no human court can discern a man's inward thoughts or desires, so they normally insist that judges should concern themselves only with what a man has said or done, and should

[1] Robert Haldane, *Epistle to the Romans* (Banner of Truth Trust, London, 1958), p. 210.

leave the evaluation of his motives and intentions to the judgment of the Omniscient – and this, again, represents a distinction which is by no means strange to writers on law and ethics.

A somewhat similar mode of thought is also characteristic of
Hinduism. Here the key to the Hindu view of life may be found,
I think, in the term *dharma*, the meaning of which comprises
(1) the 'form' of things as they are, (2) the power which keeps
them so, (3) the moral law which governs human life, and (4)
the law as this has been deduced from the sacred texts.[1]
But it is significant that a distinction is sometimes made between the *dharma* which is incumbent upon a man as a member of some particular caste, on the one hand, and the *sanātana
dharma*, or eternal law, on the other. It is the agonizing conflict which may arise between these two imperatives which
constitutes the tragic element in the mythological stories of
Arjuna and Yudhisthira; and it is certainly the *sanātana
dharma*, rather than the detailed law of caste as taught by the
Brahmins, that Gandhi and other Indian reformers have
sought to discern and apply. Precisely the same conflict sometimes arises, moreover, between the Fundamental Rights
enunciated in the Indian Constitution (which may, perhaps,
be equated with a contemporary understanding of part of this
sanātana dharma) and some of the rules and regulations of the
caste system which have been accepted by Hindus, for many
centuries, as part of a law which rests on divine revelation.
And we here encounter the further phenomenon of positive
laws, enacted by the legislature to embody this eternal law
(or these Fundamental Rights), standing over against the
religious law as previously understood.

MORALITY AND LAW IN WESTERN JURISPRUDENCE

But it is time to return from Islamic and Hindu thought to
that of the Western world. Here it is notorious that most
jurists in England or America have little time for theories of
'natural law', and concentrate almost exclusively on the posi-

---

[1] R. C. Zaehner, *Hinduism* (Oxford University Press, London, 1966),
pp. 3 and 4. The word *dharma* comes from a root which means 'to hold
together'.

tive law of statutory legislation, judicial decisions and such customary practice as is regarded as obligatory. Indeed, this attitude of mind seems to be characteristic of lawyers who live under a constitution which is accepted as basically just, or in a country and era in which the 'rule of law' normally prevails. But it seems to be equally true that when the rule of law is effectively suppressed, and when a despotic government proceeds to enact and enforce laws which are both cruel and oppressive, men's minds instinctively turn to a law of eternal validity by reference to which all positive law may be evaluated and judged.

A recent example of this phenomenon may be found in pre-Nazi and post-Nazi Germany. Before the Hitler régime German writers on jurisprudence were among the most extreme advocates of an exclusive concentration on positive law; but Radbruch was not alone in his conversion, under the pressure of Nazi tyranny, from his previous insistence that any resistance to positive law on moral grounds is exclusively a problem of the individual conscience to the view that the fundamental principles of humanitarian morality are part of the very concept of legality, and that no positive enactment which defies or ignores them can be valid. It was, indeed, the ease with which the Nazis could and did exploit an attitude of subservience to laws which were constitutional in form but vicious in content which convinced him, and many others, that there was an inherent defect in the positivist thesis. Nor was this new attitude confined to writers on jurisprudence; on the contrary, the courts themselves, in the years which followed the downfall of the Hitler régime, held that certain Nazi statutes were 'contrary to the sound conscience and sense of justice of all decent human beings', and therefore unworthy of being regarded as law. So those who relied on the provisions of one of these statutes to justify actions which would otherwise have been criminal discovered that the courts refused to accept any such defence and proceeded to punish them for their misdeeds.

This is, of course, an extreme example which almost amounts to the courts declaring certain legislation *ultra vires* the executive or legislature – in the way in which this is regularly done

C

in those countries which have a written constitution or some entrenched 'Bill of Rights'. More commonly, however, the conflict of conscience regarding some questionable enactment confronts an individual citizen rather than a court of law; and in such cases it does not make much difference whether he takes the view that the legislation concerned is so contrary to natural justice that he cannot regard it as law at all, or whether he prefers to say that the enactment, although certainly positive law, is so unjust or immoral that he cannot, and will not, obey it – and will urge others to take the same course. In either case he is evaluating the legislation concerned by reference to a standard which he regards as of greater authority, whether he calls this natural law or morality. And the very fact that we habitually criticize some laws as unjust, and commend others as fair, shows that we all have some such standard of reference, whether transcendental or otherwise.

There is, then, a clear inter-relation between law and morality, but they are by no means synonymous. It is perfectly possible for the law to be contrary to what most people would accept as natural justice and morality, and there is a whole range of moral teaching which could not possibly be given legal sanction. This is partly because the demands of morality may be said to be maximal, while the requirements of the law must be confined to what is, by comparison, minimal. Morality, for example, enjoins us to love our neighbour as ourselves; but law must content itself with trying to prevent any such speech or action as injures our neighbour's legitimate interests. Again, morality – as we have noted – concerns itself not only with what can be seen and judged by men, but also the thoughts, motives and feelings which no-one except God can know or evaluate.

Even in regard to overt acts, moreover, there must necessarily be a vast difference between morality and law. On the one hand, the law must include a large number of rules in the choice of which no moral criterion seems to be applicable – such as those which determine whether drivers of vehicles should keep to the left or right hand side of the road, or those which regulate at what point, in a contract of sale, ownership of the purchased property will pass from seller to buyer. It is certainly a concern of morality that such rules, once established, should be respected, for on this the good order of communal life depends; but there is no intrinsic moral quality in the rules *per se*. Equally, on the other hand, the law should not attempt to prohibit by legal sanctions a wide range of those types of behaviour which morality may deprecate.

The reasons for this are, in part, sufficiently obvious. It is futile, for example, for the criminal law to get seriously out of step with public opinion, whether this takes the form of lagging behind it or giving a lead which the public is not prepared to follow; for unless a law is substantially supported by the common conscience of the community it cannot be effectively enforced. Similarly, it is usually[1] a mistake to enact, or maintain, legal prohibitions the enforcement of which is clearly beyond the power of the police; for a legal requirement which is openly and continually flouted brings the law itself, and its enforcement agencies, into disrepect. There are, moreover, other criteria which are relevant to the question of the suitability, or desirability, of legal sanctions. Would an injunction or prohibition of this nature, for example, entail consequences so undesirable as to outweigh any countervailing benefit? Even if the police could enforce it, could they enforce it equitably? Would such enforcement give rise to a danger of widespread blackmail? Would it involve an unacceptable invasion of individual or family privacy? Or would it impose such a limitation on personal freedom – and thus on that liberty of choice and decision which is fundamental to moral maturity – as would represent a moral loss disproportionate to any alleged benefit to the community as a whole?

But, quite apart from these criteria, the question is often asked whether it is *ever* appropriate for morality, as such, to be enforced by the criminal law. The law should certainly intervene to prevent any unjustifiable injury to persons or property; so murder, rape, assault, arson, burglary, theft, *etc.*, are rightly treated as crimes as well as sins. Much the same may be said of demanding money by menaces (more common-

---

[1] An exception to this may, perhaps, be found in the prohibition of black-marketeering in times of crisis; for although it may be impossible for the police to enforce this prohibition, it may serve to restrict the practice.

ly called blackmail); for, however heinous the conduct of the person who is threatened may have been, both morality and law demand that this should not provide a weapon by which one man may exploit another for his own purposes – whether greed, revenge, or even a mistaken notion of what the blackmailer may regard as justice. On the same principle, the law should seek to prevent any exploitation of the young or weak, and to protect the community as a whole from grave offence to the susceptibilities of any substantial number of its members. But it has often been argued that there is a sphere of private morality which is no business of the criminal law: that what a man or woman does in private, or what two or more sane, responsible adults may agree to do in private, is exclusively their own conern.

This is the view that was taken in the Report of the Committee on Homosexual Offences and Prostitution, commonly known as the Wolfenden Report. The function of the criminal law, it states categorically, 'is to preserve public order and decency, to protect the citizen from what is offensive or injurious, and to provide sufficient safeguards against exploitation and corruption of others, particularly those who are specially vulnerable because they are young, weak in body or mind, inexperienced, or in a state of special physical, official or economic dependence'. But it was not the function of the law, the Committee considered, 'to intervene in the private lives of citizens, or to seek to enforce any particular pattern of behaviour, further than is necessary to carry out the purposes we have outlined'.[1] This represents a somewhat modified version of John Stuart Mill's famous statement of principle that 'the sole end for which mankind are warranted, individually or collectively, in interfering with the liberty of action of any of their number, is self-protection. That the only purpose for which power can be rightfully exercised over any member of a civilised community, against his will, is to prevent harm to others. His own good, either physical or moral, is not a sufficient warrant. He cannot rightfully be compelled to do or forbear because it will be better for him to do so, because it will make him happier, because, in the

[1] Paragraph 13.

opinion of others, to do so would be wise, or even right.'[1]
But it is important to note that Mill himself considered this
principle applicable only to those 'in the maturity of their
faculties' – *i.e.* not to children, or to backward societies.[2]

DEVLIN V. HART

A great deal has been written on this subject during the last
twelve years, ever since Lord Devlin took the quotation I
have cited from the Wolfenden Report as the starting-point
for his Maccabaean Lecture in 1958 on 'The Enforcement of
Morals'.[3] While he largely agreed with the practical recom-
mendations of the Wolfenden Committee regarding prostitution and homosexual offences, Lord Devlin challenged their
basic assumption that there was a sphere of private morality
which was altogether outside the purview of the criminal law.
Instead, he argued that a society is held together not only by
its political structure but also by a shared morality; and that
just as every community has the right to protect its political
integrity by the law of treason, so it has the right, in suitable
circumstances, to safeguard its ideological integrity by criminal sanctions. But this thesis – and the detailed arguments by
which Lord Devlin supported it and developed it – was almost
immediately called in question by H. L. A. Hart, who gave
general support to the views of John Stuart Mill. Since then
the debate has reverberated widely, and Hart has radically
qualified his endorsement of Mill's thesis; for he fully accepts
that the law may at times adopt a paternalistic attitude,
and may try to protect even a responsible adult from doing
something which is manifestly bad for him, however much he
may himself want to do this.

All the same, he strenuously maintains that there is an essential difference between examples of such paternalism in the
law and any attempt to enforce moral standards by criminal
sanctions; and he insists that argument on this subject is all

[1] J. S. Mill, *On Liberty* (London, 1859). Reprinted in *Utilitarianism, Liberty
and Representative Government* (J. M. Dent, London, 1910), Everyman's
Library no. 482, pp. 72f.
[2] *Ibid.*, p. 73.
[3] *Proceedings of the British Academy*, xlv. See his book of the same title (Oxford
University Press, London, 1965), chapter 1.

too often obscured by confusing these two principles and by classifying examples of paternalism as the enforcement of moral principles. Thus he would himself support legislation designed to prevent even responsible adults from obtaining free access to hard drugs, on the grounds that such drugs are a demonstrable danger to health and all too swiftly lead to addiction. This is almost certainly the example of paternalism which can most easily be defended on his premises. But he would also argue that a criminal sanction for a bigamous marriage, even where both parties are fully cognizant of all the circumstances, can be justified in terms of the offence that would be caused to the sensibilities of many members of the community by the desecration of a solemn service in church – or, presumably, a similar ceremony in a registry office – by using it to perpetrate a hollow deception. Yet again, he would explain the fact that under English law the consent of the victim is frequently no defence to a criminal charge, *not* in terms of the moral principle of the sanctity of life or the physical integrity of the person,[1] but as another example of paternalism – however repugnant this would have been to Mill. Where, on the other hand, the criminal law includes provisions which can be explained only in terms of what he regards as an attempt to enforce morality as such – *e.g.* 'laws against various forms of homosexual behaviour between males, sodomy between persons of different sex even if married, bestiality, incest, living on the earnings of prostitution, keeping a house for prostitution, and also, since the decision in Shaw's case, a conspiracy to corrupt public morals'[2] (interpreted to mean leading others, in the opinion of a jury, 'morally astray') – these should, in his view, be totally expunged.

The weakness in this argument seems to me obvious. If it is permissible to promulgate laws which are frankly paternalistic, where, precisely, must we draw the line? Is a man to be protected in this way only against such physical harm as he would otherwise inflict on himself or allow someone else to inflict upon him? But why should not laws designed to prevent the

[1] H. L. A. Hart, *Law, Liberty and Morality* (Oxford University Press, London, 1963), pp. 30–34, 28, 25–26.
[2] *Ibid.*, p. 25.

infliction of moral harm be regarded as an equally permissible form of paternalism? The answer some would give is that the injury done to physical health by hard drugs is demonstrable and undeniable, whereas the moral harm which incest or living on the earnings of prostitution, for example, do to the individuals concerned, or to the body politic, is more questionable. But is it? Does the difference consist only in the fact that physical injury can be more easily proved and quantified than moral harm? This may be conceded. Or is the basic assumption that the damage which drugs may cause to physical health cannot be gainsaid, whereas what is commonly regarded as moral evil amounts to no more than a deviation, which in fact 'causes harm to no one', from accepted norms which are themselves relative and questionable?

If this is the basis of the argument, there is a great deal to be said on the other side. Why, for example, is it a matter of common agreement that the criminal law should provide 'sufficient safeguards against exploitation and corruption of others, particularly those who are specially vulnerable because they are young, weak in body or mind, inexperienced, or in a state of special physical, official or economic dependence' (to revert to the Report of the Wolfenden Committee quoted above)? The idea behind these words clearly goes beyond an 'exploitation' which consists in nothing more than an inducement to agree to a proposal which, had they been older, stronger or less dependent, they might possibly have refused, for the word 'exploitation' is immediately followed by 'corruption'. This clearly implies that there *is* such a thing as moral corruption and that certain acts or behaviour are liable to cause it. Is it, then, suggested that behaviour which tends to corrupt the young, the weak and the dependent – or even 'backward societies' (to revert to Mill) – has no such effect on the mature, the strong, the independent and the civilized? Or is the argument, on the contrary, that this behaviour is liable to corrupt people of any age or condition, but that those who are not especially vulnerable to exploitation must be allowed to submit themselves to such corruption – or at least the possibility of such corruption – if they so wish?

It should, I think, be observed in passing that to live on the

earnings of prostitution must often involve the exploitation of
one who is 'specially vulnerable', at least by reason of some
kind of dependence. There is, indeed, at least something to
be said for the much wider contention of Lord Devlin that
both the prostitute herself and her clients mutually exploit
each other's moral weakness; and much the same could be
said about homosexual practices, incest, the peddling of pornography, or the advertisement of facilities for sexual indulgence
of one sort or another. It seems to me significant that Hart
himself, when he sets out to explain why he cannot regard
restrictions on the free purchase of drugs as an unwarrantable
interference with the liberty of choice of a responsible, civilized adult, remarks that our lack of sympathy today with
Mill's view is no doubt 'due, in part, to a general decline in
the belief that individuals know their own interests best, and
to an increased awareness of a great range of factors which
diminish the significance to be attached to an apparently
free choice or to consent. Choices may be made or consent
given without adequate reflection or appreciation of the
consequences; or in pursuit of merely transitory desires; or
in various predicaments when the judgment is likely to be
clouded; or under inner psychological compulsion; or under
pressure by others of a kind too subtle to be susceptible of proof
in a law court. Underlying Mill's extreme fear of paternalism
there is perhaps a conception of what a normal human being
is like which now seems not to correspond to the facts.'[1]

Precisely; the paternalism appropriate to the young, weak
and dependent, and to 'backward societies', cannot properly
be confined to them alone. So we come back once more to
the question of how we define the concept of 'causing harm',
either to oneself or another, and whether this can, or cannot,
properly be held to include moral harm. Can we really speak,
in any general and meaningful way, about acts which 'deviate
from accepted morality but harm no one'?[2]

It is noteworthy that the distinction between what is 'moral'

[1] *Ibid.*, pp. 32f. The import of this passage has, I think, received too little
attention in a valuable article on 'Crime and Immorality' by C. L. Ten,
in *The Modern Law Review*, 1969, pp. 648ff.
[2] *Ibid.*, p. 57.

and what is 'immoral' is inherent in our civil as well as our criminal law, for a contract designed to provide for, or facilitate, some immoral activity is wholly unenforceable before the courts. This means that banner headlines such as 'Homosexual practices legalized', which greeted the Sexual Offences Act 1967, were at best misleading. The Act did not in fact 'legalize' such behaviour, for it is still regarded by the law as immoral and is devoid of any legal recognition; all the Act did was to remove the criminal sanction from such acts when performed in private between two adult and consenting males, and thus put them on a par with lesbian practices on the part of two females – which were not subject to criminal sanctions even prior to 1967, although they would always have been treated as immoral. But the same Act considerably *increased* the penalties applicable to an adult male who exploits in this way a youth who has not reached the age of 21 – not because such behaviour would do him physical injury, but because it is still regarded as immoral and tending to corrupt him, or lead him 'morally astray'. It is noteworthy, moreover, that Mill himself found it impossible to decide whether an adult member of a civilized society should be free to be a pimp or to keep a gambling house. This would seem an almost inevitable deduction from his basic principles; but he saw much force in the contrary argument that 'if society believes conduct to be bad, it must be at least a disputable question whether it is good or bad: that being so, society is entitled to exclude the influence of solicitations which are not disinterested'.[1] But this concession seems to undermine the logical consistency of his whole thesis. A responsible adult must, he insists, be permitted to indulge, whether alone or with others, in conduct which the 'public' believes to be morally wrong; he must be allowed himself to peddle pornography (or a woman to offer her body), it would seem, even for financial gain; and he must also be permitted to persuade others to indulge in such conduct, whatever his motives or methods (provided, of course, these do not amount to coercion) – except only that if it is for financial gain that he puts people into contact with each other

[1] P. A. Devlin, *The Enforcement of Morals* (Oxford University Press, London 1965), p. 108. *Cf.* Mill, *op. cit.*, pp. 154f.

for such purposes, or runs a gambling house, brothel, or premises which purvey indecent shows, then (and then only) there are, it appears, respectable arguments for making him liable to criminal sanctions.

THE INDIVIDUAL AND SOCIETY

Nor can we confine this question to the protection of individuals, for the protection of the well-being of society as a whole, and of its basic institutions, is equally relevant. Here the obvious examples are those of marriage and the family, for these are regulated, in one way or another, in every community. A society may, of course, be polygamous or monogamous, or even both; but it is clear that the structure of the family and society in the Western world is firmly based on monogamy. Why, therefore, should not the law be invoked – in appropriate circumstances and with suitable safeguards – to protect this structure? Many criteria must be fulfilled, as we have already seen, before it is appropriate to impose criminal sanctions; so in the contemporary world adultery or fornication are seldom punished as such. But it is one thing not to *prosecute* a man or woman who cohabits with a number of different partners, and quite another to recognize polygamous unions as valid, legal marriages.

What attitude should we take, then, towards the assertion of the House of Lords in the case of *Shaw* v. *Director of Public Prosecutions* that the courts are still *custodes morum* and that they still have a 'residual power, where no statute has yet intervened to supersede the common law, to superintend those offences which are prejudicial to the public welfare'?[1] The danger in conceding such a position to the courts is obvious, for it involves the sacrifice of the basic principle of legality which requires that criminal offences should be defined as precisely as possible, and that it should be known in advance, with reasonable certainty, whether a certain course of action will be regarded as criminal. But Lord Simonds insisted that it necessarily takes time for Parliament to intervene, and that there will always, therefore, be gaps in the law, 'since no one can foresee every way in which the wickedness of man may

[1] Per Lord Simonds. 2 A.E.R. at pp. 452–453, (1962) AC at p. 268.

disrupt the order of society'. Even when Parliament does intervene, moreover, the definition of such offences as obscenity and indecency is so difficult that a great deal must necessarily be left to the discretion of the courts.

But obscenity is not only difficult to define; it is still more difficult to prove, according to the legal, rather than the dictionary, definition of that which will 'tend to deprave and corrupt persons who are likely, having regard to all the relevant circumstances, to read, see or hear it'. All the same, in 1968 the police seized as 'obscene' more than 26,000 books and photographs, and brought criminal charges against 132 persons; the General Post Office stopped 6,000 postal packets, and launched 21 successful prosecutions involving 4,630 photographs; and the Customs officers seized 792,000 magazines and 703,000 books.[1] In the overwhelming majority of cases, moreover, the material concerned was so obviously pornographic, with no redeeming features, that the action of police, Post Office or Customs went unchallenged – and I think it would be a bold man who would assert that this action represented a wrong and repressive infringement of human liberty, or that it caused any harm whatever except to those who purveyed the items concerned for financial gain. It is where a book, magazine, photograph or play has some pretensions to literary, artistic or scientific merit that a problem arises; for under the law as it now stands it is not only notoriously difficult to get a conviction, but the publicity which the trial receives is apt to turn what might otherwise have been almost unnoticed into a best seller or box office success.[2]

The fact that a positive galaxy of distinguished witnesses seem to be prepared to testify to the literary, artistic or scientific value of a book or play which would otherwise be banned

[1] *Cf. Obscene Publications: Law and Practice* (Board of Social Responsibility of the General Synod of the Church of England, 1970), p. 8.
[2] This is largely because the Obscene Publications Act, 1959, expressly provides that, even though a person publishes or holds for gain an obscene article, he can still avoid conviction if he can prove 'that the publication of the article . . . is justified as being for the public good on the ground that it is in the interests of science, literature, art, or learning, or of other objects of general concern'.

as pornographic can, I think, often be explained in terms of their fundamental objection to anything that savours of censorship rather than any realistic appraisal of the case in point.[1] Nor can I see why the fact that an author betrays a certain artistic ability should save the whole of a book in which he gratuitously includes quite unnecessarily offensive passages. In such cases his artistic talent might well increase, rather than mitigate, the demoralizing effect of such passages – if such material does in fact have any influence on the moral climate of society or on the actual behaviour of individuals. But in so far as society is concerned, the dictum of an American judge that 'over a long period of time the indiscriminate dissemination of materials, the essential character of which is to degrade sex, will have an eroding influence on moral standards'[2] would appear to be a reasonable inference. It is much more difficult, of course, to assess the influence of pornography on the actual conduct of individuals; but it seems to me beyond reasonable doubt that this largely depends on the persons concerned. To some – perhaps the majority – such material will prove both boring and disgusting, and may even serve to quench any prurient curiosity. But in others pornography and sadism may well provoke or feed fantasies which are, at best, immature and unhealthy, and may, at worst, suddenly erupt in giving concrete expression to what has been festering in the mind.

In saying this, I am not primarily referring to erotica of the sort which do not involve sadism or tend to cheapen sex: erotica, that is, which do not divorce the physical side of sex from the personality and true feelings of those concerned.

[1] In its narrower sense, the term 'censorship' should, I think, be reserved for the suppression of, or making of incisions or changes in, a play, film, book or other material *before* it is shown or published. But the term is also frequently used, as here, to cover any action taken against a play or book *subsequently*. Censorship (in an intermediate sense) exercised under our present law by the Customs, Post Office, *etc.*, would seem to be beneficial – subject always to a right of appeal; but in general it would appear preferable to rely not so much on prior 'censorship' (which might so easily be abused for political reasons), as on the subsequent prosecution of those who transgress the law. But there is an urgent need today for a much more satisfactory formulation of the relevant legal provisions – a discussion of which lies beyond the scope of this chapter.

[2] 'Sex and Morals 1954–63', in *The Criminal Law Review*, April 1964.

Our sexuality is, in itself, one of God's best gifts, and it is both wrong and misleading to give any contrary impression. Even so, there are obvious dangers in a treatment of sex which gives the impression that *any* upsurge of genuine affection may rightly be given physical expression, or that to give such expression to feelings of romantic love outside marriage is more 'moral' than intimacy inside a marriage which has lost its initial romance. It is also true, I think, that for many people the problem is not so much to awaken a sex instinct which is deficient or quiescent as to restrain one which tends to be too pervasive.

A moral restraint which is self-imposed, or even exercised by public opinion, is certainly preferable to legal sanctions; and no law which would be acceptable can do more than seek to penalize – and thus discourage – anything which goes beyond the bounds of what public opinion regards as tolerable. But I have already remarked that it might be preferable, in so far as the stage is concerned, to abandon the criterion of what tends to 'deprave and corrupt' for the rather simpler standard of what is offensive – a criterion which would, I should have thought, exclude the performance, or realistic simulation, of the sex act or its perversions, masturbation, or any vulgar exploitation of nudity. Such displays may be difficult to prohibit in Soho – although I should have thought that much more than is at present attempted could have been done even in this respect – but could surely be excluded from the regular theatre or the television screen, whether on the grounds of the moral harm they are likely to do or, in terms of Hart's principles, of the offence they cause to responsible members of the public. This principle would also be applicable to advertisements, hoardings or displays of books or pictures likely to prove offensive to any considerable section of the community – or, of course, to arouse racial antipathies. Much the same considerations apply to any form of sadism or cruelty; and pressure is building up today against both coursing and stag hunting, for example, on the grounds that it is immoral to inflict unnecessary suffering on animals in the name of sport. But it is interesting to note that it is often those who are most permissive in some matters who are themselves most restrictive in others; so it seems clear that what chiefly concerns them is not so much the abstract principle of unrestricted liberty as the sphere of activity concerned.

THE INTERDEPENDENCE OF MORALITY AND LAW

There can be no manner of doubt, moreover, that morality and law reinforce each other's authority. They represent 'two forms of social control aimed at preventing certain injurious consequences. In some cases the one kind of control, in some the other will be the more appropriate and each is necessary to the other'.[1] The debt which the law owes to morality is evident from the fact that most people are deeply distressed at the very thought of being convicted of a crime which involves moral obloquy, but will accept conviction and punishment for the breach of some statutory regulation with comparative equanimity. Without this moral reinforcement the law would play a much less effective role in the control of communal life, for the vast majority of people obey its injunctions because of its moral authority rather than fear of the consequences which may – or may not – follow its breach. It is important, therefore, that the moral authority of the law should not be eroded by the continual multiplication of statutory offences which have little or no ethical basis.

The debt owed by morality to the law, on the other hand, is somewhat less obvious, for it can be argued that a morality which is induced by nothing higher than the fear of legal sanctions is unworthy of the name. It has even been questioned whether the enforcement of morality is itself morally justified.[2] But it can scarcely be denied that the fact that some act is criminally punishable as well as morally wrong may on occasion reinforce the resistance of one who might otherwise have succumbed to temptation – which may, in its turn, strengthen his moral fibre; and it seems equally clear that the fact that certain behaviour has been declared illegal and made subject to criminal sanctions will sometimes, at least, have a substan-

[1] Basil Mitchell, *Law, Morality and Religion* (Oxford University Press, London, 1967), p. 74.
[2] *Cf.* H. L. A. Hart, *op. cit.*, p. 17.

tial influence on the way in which such behaviour is regarded
by the community. It is, indeed, for this reason that Morris
Ginsberg remarked that American legislation designed to
prevent and penalize segregation might well, if persistently
enforced, 'help to bring about a change in attitude, in behaviour and eventually in moral convictions'.[1] Precisely the same
is true, I think, of our own Race Relations Acts – to say nothing
of the fact that they make it considerably easier for a well-
disposed employer, for example, to resist pressure from those
who seek to oppose a just and liberal policy.

It is, of course, an extremely complex and controversial
problem to know at what point the criminal law should intervene. Mill himself was utterly opposed to a 'selfish indif-
ference which pretends that human beings have no business
with each others' conduct in life and that they should not
concern themselves about the well-doing or well-being of one
another . . . Human beings owe to each other help to distinguish the better from the worse and encouragement to choose
the former and avoid the latter'.[2] He approved of arguments
and exhortations designed to aid another's judgment and
strengthen his will, of warnings of the distaste and contempt
to which certain conduct gives rise, and even of social ostrac-
ism. But there must, in his view, be no coercion; the individual must remain 'the final judge' of his moral conduct. So,
too, Michael Keeling, who approaches the subject from a very
different standpoint, maintains that 'the highest aim of the
law is the protection of the individual. To say otherwise is to
misunderstand the whole basis of morals, for the primary
principle of moral action is that it is free action – and this
necessarily implies some freedom to make and carry out wrong
moral choices'.[3] For love, as he says elsewhere, 'requires
that we allow other people the responsibility of deciding their
own actions, even when this leads to decisions of which we
disapprove'.[4]

This is perfectly true so far as it goes; and it represents the

[1] M. Ginsberg, *On Justice in Society* (Penguin Books, Harmondsworth, 1965),
p. 235.
[2] Quoted by Hart, *op. cit.*, p. 76.
[3] M. Keeling, *Morals in a Free Society* (SCM Press, London, 1967), p. 57.
[4] *Ibid.*, p. 105.

attitude which God himself seems normally to take towards
his creatures. But there are very few moral choices which have
no effect whatever on anyone other than the one who takes
them – whether we think in terms of specific third parties or of
society as a whole. We can illustrate this, I think, in relation
to such questions as abortion, euthanasia and divorce. To
refuse an abortion when the mother's life or health, whether
of body or mind, is genuinely at risk, seems to me utterly
wrong; for surely the well-being of a *developed* human personality must be given precedence over that of a *potential* human
personality? But I cannot believe that to treat the mother 'as
a responsible human being, capable of making her own moral
decisions', in Keeling's words, means that she should be
allowed to demand the removal of a foetus as though it were
no more than a tumour; for here our fundamental attitude
to the sanctity of life – and the interests of both the foetus
and society as well as those of the mother – are involved. But
the decision whether an abortion is, or is not, justified must,
in the nature of the case, be taken by the medical profession;
so it is wrong, in my view, to introduce any criteria which
are outside a doctor's competence. Thus a doctor is not
fitted to evaluate social considerations as such, or even –
in most cases – to decide whether the pregnancy was, or was
not, the result of rape; but the age of the patient, the circumstances in which she conceived, the fear that the child may be
malformed, and the total situation in which she finds herself, may all be highly relevant factors in a medical assessment of the danger that the continuation of the pregnancy
may be to her mental or physical health. The problem is to
find a form of words which will allow conscientious doctors
this latitude of discretion without opening the door to widespread abuse by either the more unscrupulous or permissive
members of the profession.

So, too, with regard to euthanasia. It seems to me clearly
right for a doctor to use whatever drugs may be needed to
relieve pain, even when he knows that a side effect of their
use will be to shorten the life of the sufferer; and I see no
reason whatever why he should employ what may be termed
artificial means to prolong the act of dying. But I cannot be-

lieve that he should go so far as deliberately to bring life to an end – except, I suppose, in the case of a baby so malformed as to be scarcely recognizable as a human being. If doctors were permitted (and willing) to put an abrupt end to the life of the old and sick at the request of their family, what confidence would remain between doctor and patient? And if the patient's own request is to be the criterion, how can anyone be sure that he might not have changed his mind next week? As for divorce, there seem to me several objections to leaving the decision exclusively to the husband and wife as 'responsible human beings'; for to open the door to 'divorce by consent' not only ignores the interests of any children of the marriage, but also the interests of society in attempting to ensure that marriage represents what is at least intended to be a lasting partnership, and not an experimental relationship which may be of exceedingly brief duration. So it should be left to the courts, rather than the whim of the parties, to terminate a marriage – preferably by way of giving a decent burial to a union which is already, as it appears, dead and meaningless.

To sum up. It seems to me that the problem of when the law should intrude in matters which are *primarily* of moral import can be solved only by attempting to strike a series of balances between competing interests. First, there is the balance between the interests of the individual or individuals primarily concerned and those of other people who are in some measure involved, or the broader interests of society as a whole. Again, there is the balance between the good an enactment might do, if it could be satisfactorily administered, and the evil which would result from a law which could not be adequately or equitably enforced, or which gave rise to unacceptable side-effects. Yet again, there is the balance between the basic value inherent in the liberty of moral choice exercised by a responsible human being and what may be termed a legitimate paternalism designed to protect him from choices which would cause him serious harm – whether physical, psychological, economic or moral.

But this brings us back to our basic dilemma: the criterion by which we can decide such a controversial problem as the nature of moral harm. In questions of sexual morality, for example, are we really left with nothing more convincing than a matter of 'variable tastes and conventions', as Hart asserts? It is significant that he himself frankly admits that the position would be very different if we could find some principles which 'had the status of divine commands or of eternal truth discovered by reason' – although he adds, somewhat gratuitously, that this 'would not for obvious reasons now seem plausible'.[1] But I have already argued, in my last chapter, that this is not nearly as impossible as he imagines. There seem to me to be excellent reasons for believing that the teaching of Christ had unique and divine authority, and that he himself endorsed the basic moral teaching of the Old Testament and extended his own authority, by implication, to that given subsequently by the apostles. Not only so, but I believe that there are valid arguments, even outside Scripture, which demonstrate that this basic moral teaching represents what is beneficial to society – or, as I would put it, the 'Maker's instructions' as to how his creatures can best enjoy the life he designed them to live. It is on such grounds that this teaching – and, where appropriate, legislation based on it – can be commended to non-Christians in a pluralistic democracy.

[1] H. L. A. Hart, *op. cit.*, pp. 73f.

4 MORALITY AND LAW II
The problem of tyranny and injustice

In my last chapter I discussed, in general terms, the relationship and interaction between morality and law. We saw that there is an essential connection between these two methods of regulating human conduct, yet an equally inevitable distinction and difference. In the course of that argument we noted, moreover, that positive law may, on occasion, depart quite radically from the dictates of morality – even to the point where some particular enactment is considered to be so contrary to natural justice that men deny that it has any right to be regarded as law at all. And what may be true of a single enactment or decision of the courts may also, of course, apply to the administration of justice as a whole, for situations frequently arise in which the 'Rule of Law' itself may be said not yet – or no longer – to prevail.

SHOULD TYRANNY BE RESISTED?

What, then, does morality require of men who find themselves face to face with unjust laws, an inequitable administration of justice, or an oppressive and tyrannical government? Is it permissible – or even, perhaps, obligatory – in such circumstances to disobey the law and defy the government, or must the law and the government, just or unjust, always be obeyed? What means, if any, may be taken to get an unjust law changed or to overthrow a tyrannical government? Where constitutional attempts to do this have proved abortive, should resistance always be restricted to passive disobedience, or may active steps be taken to induce social change? May such action fever involve violence, bloodshed or even tyrannicide? Is there in fact a doctrine of a 'Just Revolution' – a revolution in which even convinced Christians may consistently, with good conscience, participate?

There can be no manner of doubt about the relevance and urgency of these questions today. This is not only, or even primarily, because injustice is now more widespread or palpable than it was in the past. On the contrary, although manifest and grievous injustices unquestionably disfigure the face of our contemporary world, it would be a bold man who would assert that the situation is any worse today than it has all too often been in the past. Circumstances do, inevitably, change from age to age; one injustice is, in part, remedied, and another takes its place; but the fact remains that 'the dark places of the earth' – and also the not quite so dark places – are still 'full of the habitations of cruelty'. What has changed radically in our age and generation is the fact that injustice is no longer generally accepted as the inevitable and irremediable lot of man. Instead, today it provokes questioning and opposition, demonstrations and organized resistance, and a somewhat facile doctrine of revolt and anarchy.

This necessarily poses our problem from two diametrically opposite points of view. We have already asked whether there are not circumstances in which disobedience to authority is not permissible or even obligatory, in which a government may be so unjust that steps may legitimately be taken to overthrow it, or in which revolution may not provide the only possible solution. But we must equally ask ourselves whether there are not circumstances in which injustice may not have to be borne, in which peaceful and constitutional means of effecting social change are alone permissible, or in which – however tyrannical the government, however oppressive the executive, however unjust the laws and inequitable their enforcement by the judiciary – violent revolution must not be regarded as the worst evil of all.

The two passages in the New Testament which deal most explicitly with the duty owed by citizens to their government are Romans 13:1–7 and 1 Peter 2:13–17.[1] Both, at first sight,

[1] The argument in the next four or five pages is closely similar to that in *Civil Strife* (Board of Social Responsibility of the General Synod of the

appear to teach that every government, whatever its nature, is divinely ordained, and that the 'powers that be' invariably have the right to claim our obedience and respect. Anyone who rebels against authority is, therefore, 'resisting a divine institution'. But the seemingly unqualified injunctions of the first two verses of Romans 13 must, presumably, be read in the light of the next two verses, which state that those who 'continue to do right' need have no fear whatev er o governmental authorities, which are 'God's agents working for your good'. It is only wrongdoers, we are told, who stand in any jeopardy. Similarly, in 1 Peter 2, while verse 19 teaches that for the individual Christian patiently to endure harsh and inequitable treatment is praiseworthy before God, verse 14 explicitly describes a governor as God's 'deputy for the punishment of criminals and the commendation of those who do right'. In other words, the God-given function of secular authority is to discourage social evil (whether by education, legislation or even criminal sanctions) and to encourage social good (by every available means, including civil honours and awards). If, therefore, this situation is turned upside down – if the government becomes so corrupt that vicious laws are promulgated and enforced, corrupt officials put in authority and the innocent made to suffer – then it is distinctly arguable that the obligation of obedience no longer applies, at least in its entirety.[1]

This attitude is often challenged by reference to the example of Christ and his apostles. Jesus himself, we are reminded, took no active steps to abolish slavery or to resist the authority of alien rulers. On the contrary, he rejected the way of the

---

Church of England, 1971), the Report of a Working Party of which I had the honour to act as chairman.

[1] The objection commonly made to this reasoning is that these two New Testament passages were written in the reign of the tyrant Nero. But there are several indications, I think, that they were written before the era of formal, fierce persecution. How else could the apostles have written Rom. 13:3 and 4; 1 Pet. 2:14; 3:13, 14 and 17; 4:16, *etc.*? The dates when these Epistles were written are, of course, a matter of controversy and do not, in any case, alter the basic teaching; the significance of the date lies in the question whether such verses as Rom. 13:3 and 4 and 1 Pet. 2:14 can be regarded as applying to a time not merely of autocracy but of such tyranny and injustice as to reverse the God-given functions of government.

Zealots and deliberately chose the way of the cross.[1] And his disciples, for the most part, seem to have followed his example and to have limited their defiance of authority to those circumstances in which it came into direct conflict with what they regarded as unequivocal divine commands.

It must always be remembered, however, that Jesus himself had a wholly unique mission to fulfil. He was primarily concerned to change men's characters rather than the political régimes under which they lived; to transform their attitudes rather than their circumstances; to treat the sicknesses of their hearts rather than the injustices of their environment. Above all, he had come not primarily to teach, but to die; for his basic mission was to bear in his own person the sin of the world, and so to reconcile lost humanity with the God who always loves and longs to win, but who cannot ignore the sin which inevitably separates man from fellowship with himself. And while his disciples could have no part in this unique work of redemption, they too would not let anything deflect them from the all-important commission he had given them to make this redemption known. To have attempted to persuade the Roman emperor to institute social reforms was, obviously, out of the question; and to have set out to achieve reform by force would not only have been doomed to inevitable failure but have obscured, and even frustrated, their basic message of salvation.

Yet the ethical teaching of Jesus himself, together with its apostolic expansion and application, was the axe laid at the root of the tree – which was bound, ultimately, to lead to the abolition of slavery, for example, and the challenge of injustice in any form. It is the abiding shame of the Christian church that it took such an unconscionable time to assimilate the implications of his teaching, to embody them in its own conduct and to propagate them throughout the world – indeed, that it has not fully risen to its privileges and responsibilities in this regard even yet. Yet Jesus himself did not hesitate to refer to Herod as 'that fox'; to overthrow the tables of the money-changers; and to demarcate, in a single pregnant aphorism, the limited sphere of duty we all owe to the State.

[1] *Pace* S. G. F. Brandon. See below.

It is clear, moreover, that the apostles, following the teaching of their Master, refused an obedience to man which came into conflict with their obedience to God. It has, of course, been argued in this context that Peter's defiance of authority was on a specifically 'religious' issue and should not be taken as any justification for extending such defiance to 'secular' matters. But can it really be accepted that a 'secular' law which runs directly counter to divinely revealed moral injunctions, or their necessary implications, should be regarded as a matter in which we must obey 'Caesar' rather than God? It is significant, I think, that Paul, on more than one occasion, insisted that the Roman authorities should fulfil their God-appointed task of upholding the rule of law; indeed, he may even be said to have been responsible for the first recorded Christian 'sit-in' in the cause of social justice![1] As T. M. Taylor puts it: 'the obedience which the Christian man owes to the State is never absolute but, at the most, partial and contingent. It follows that the Christian lives always in a tension between two competing claims; that in certain circumstances disobedience to the command of the State may be not only a right but also a duty.'[2]

Nor is God imprisoned by the church. In the Old Testament he is frequently said to have intervened in judgment and to have overthrown unjust and oppressive rulers, sometimes by the hand of godless men. But he is also depicted as intervening in deliverance when men turned to him in penitence, not infrequently by empowering them to act decisively, and even in violent revolt, to effect their own liberation. Examples could be multiplied, but one remembers at once verses like 'Thus says the Lord to Cyrus his anointed, Cyrus whom he has taken by the hand to subdue nations before him and undo the might of kings';[3] or 'for crime after crime of Gaza I will grant them no reprieve, because they deported a whole band of exiles and delivered them up to Edom. Therefore will I send fire upon the walls or Gaza . . . I will turn my hand against Ekron, and the remnant of the Philistines shall perish.

[1] Acts 16:37.
[2] T. M. Taylor, *The Heritage of the Reformation* (St. Andrew's Press, Edinburgh, 1960), pp. 8f.   [3] Is. 45:1.

It is the word of the Lord God.'[1] One remembers also Eglon king of Moab and Ehud the Benjamite;[2] the Midianites and Gideon;[3] King Rehoboam and Jeroboam;[4] King Jehoram and the judgment that came upon both him and Jezebel at the hand of Jehu;[5] and many verses in the book of Daniel such as 'Thereby the living will know that the Most High is sovereign in the kingdom of men: he gives the kingdom to whom he will and he may set over it the humblest of mankind'.[6]

It seems clear, therefore, that the teaching of the Bible as a whole is that God is the Lord of history who not infrequently intervenes in judgment or deliverance; that at times he acts in a direct and manifestly supernatural way, but more often through the agency of men commissioned for the purpose; and that both judgment and deliverance frequently involve violence. It is also noteworthy that the Old Testament at times depicts wars, rebellions and even acts of tyrannicide as divinely inspired. And while, at first sight, the New Testament would seem to give teaching which is much more pietistic in nature, we get a somewhat different impression from such passages as 2 Thessalonians 2:5–12 or much of the book of Revelation. To argue that the Lord of history may – and indeed does – sometimes intervene in judgment, but that he must always do this by the hand of unbelievers, seems an unwarranted assumption. It is true, of course, that there was a strong pacifist emphasis in the early church, and that pacifist teaching has persisted – and represents an honoured tradition – right down the centuries. Occasionally this takes the form of the assertion that violence can never be justified, whatever the circumstances and whoever the participants may be. More often, perhaps, a distinction is made between the minimum of violence to which a police force must sometimes be compelled to resort, on the one hand, and war or armed rebellion, on the other. A still more frequent attitude, I think, is to assert, with writers such as Jacques Ellul,[7] that while violence is endemic in this fallen

---

[1] Amos 1:6–8.   [2] Jdg. 3:12–28.   [3] Jdg. 6 and 7.
[4] 1 Ki. 11:11–13, 29–37; 12:1–20; 2 Ch. 11:1–4.
[5] 1 Ki. 19:16; 2 Ki. 9.   [6] Dn. 4:17.
[7] Cf. J. Ellul, Violence: Reflections from a Christian Perspective (SCM Press, London, 1970).

world, whether from governments or those who are driven to react against them, the role of the Christian as such must always be that of the one who speaks out against evil, whatever the cost; who suffers violence, but never inflicts it; who always seeks to fulfil a ministry of reconciliation; and who leaves all judgment to an omnipotent God.

There is, indeed, a good deal in the New Testament which could be – and, of course, frequently is – cited in support of this attitude; but these citations never seem to me wholly convincing. Their immediate context appears to be that of the individual in his personal relationships: slaves with cruel masters, for example, or anyone who is subjected to insult or assault by another, whatever the circumstances may be. But it is far from obvious that they are intended to teach that the Christian must stand idly by while a woman is raped or a child butchered. If, moreover, the verses which are often quoted by convinced pacifists are to be applied literally to all situations, they would preclude a Christian from many forms of participation in secular life – as a policeman, magistrate, judge or member of a detachment of troops designed to keep the peace between Egypt and Israel, for example.

But if law and order must, in fact, be maintained – and this is a basic function of secular government, according to the clear teaching of the New Testament – then why should Christians be precluded from taking any part in what must be regarded as a corporate civic duty? If a peace-keeping force is needed in order to prevent widespread misery and bloodshed, why should Christians always contract out? Such a force would be meaningless unless it had the capacity to defend itself and fulfil its mission; so it can scarcely be argued that a Christian may consent to serve in this force but must not obey any order to fire should matters come to the crunch! War is always evil *per se*, we must all agree, and modern war more evil and calamitous than it has ever been in the past; but is it always, and inevitably, the very worst thing that can happen? Are there no situations whatever in which one must decide that violence – at least to some degree – is the lesser of two evils? And if this be so, then should a Christian always leave this most distasteful choice of the 'lesser evil' to others?

Is this really compatible with the basic injunction that we must love our neighbour as ourselves?

CAN THERE BE A 'JUST REVOLUTION'?

It is on some such basis as this that the doctrine of the 'Just War' was developed and has occupied a largely unchallenged place in Christian thought from Augustine and Aquinas until comparatively recently. For our purpose the basic criteria may, perhaps, be summarized as follows: the war must be for a just cause; it must represent the only available means of restoring justice or preventing the continuance of injustice; it must be conducted with no more violence than is absolutely necessary; and it must be waged in the reasonable expectation that the good to be obtained is greater than the certain evils, material and moral, that it must necessarily entail. But how far, it must be asked, can these principles still be regarded as relevant in the atomic age? And to this there can, I think, be only one answer. It is beyond dispute that the maxim about using no more violence than is absolutely necessary can have little or no *tactical* relevance in regard to saturation bombing or the use of atomic weapons, where no proper distinction can be made between combatants and non-combatants and no limit put to the extent of the destruction and suffering involved; although even here it has, I suppose, a certain relevance to the *strategic* decision as to whether such bombing, or the use of such weapons, is itself necessary or justified. But it is equally obvious that unless the danger of a possible escalation of a local or conventional war into an atomic holocaust is to be regarded as conclusive proof that *any* other horror, suffering or injustice must today be accepted as demonstrably preferable to incurring such a risk, then we must cling to the doctrine of the Just War, in so far as this still remains applicable, as infinitely better than a facile surrender to wholly unlimited and unprincipled butchery. The extent to which those who state that the doctrine is now obsolete and irrelevant do, in practice, still invoke many of its maxims, seems to me significant.

The complex and agonizing problems of international war are, however, outside the scope of our present consideration, except in so far as they may be applicable to rebellion and civil strife. But the question inevitably arises as to whether it is possible to work out a doctrine, or even a theology, of the 'Just Revolution'. It is obvious, I should have thought, that many of the criteria applicable to a war between nation and nation would be equally relevant to civil war between two factions in a single country, but with the proviso that there is a very real sense in which no war is more terrible, or likely to occasion more present anguish and future bitterness, than one between brothers. So can such a war ever be right?

Under constitutional law a revolution against a lawful government must always, *ex hypothesi*, be illegal, but it is interesting to note that there is a palpable difference when we turn to international law. Under the latter rebels may be recognized as 'belligerents' both by the lawful government itself and also by other States; so it may be said that international law recognizes, within limits, a right of revolution. But, however this may be, it would seem obvious that a civil war would not be ethically justifiable unless the criteria applicable to a 'just' international war were amply satisfied. There are, moreover, Christians who would not exclude the possibility of taking part in a 'just war' against an alien power, but would feel that any participation in an armed revolt against one's own lawful government could never be justified. But this involves an over-simplification of the issues. What, precisely, is a 'lawful government', and when does a government which comes to power after a *coup d'état* become 'lawful'? What is the position when one's 'own government' co-operates with an alien power, as did the Vichy French with the Germans? Would an almost bloodless *coup* such as unseated Nkruma never be justified? And can this whole line of argument really be sustained, particularly by anyone who takes the Old Testament precedents seriously, if one's 'own government' radically departs from its God-given functions?

The first essential for a 'Just Revolution' is that there must be a 'just cause', which virtually amounts to the same thing as saying that this must be the 'only available means of restoring justice or preventing the continuance of injustice'. And this, in its turn, must mean that every constitutional

method of effecting social change has been attempted, but
without success, or that constitutional methods are, in all the
circumstances, unavailable or non-existent. Where it is possible to effect a change of law by means other than force –
by propaganda, the ballot box, or (where suitable) by demonstrations and protests – there can be no justification whatever
for a resort to violence. Even so, of course, problems abound.
What, for example, is the precise definition of violence? Is a
demonstration 'violent' if the intention of the demonstrators
themselves is peaceable, but if they know that their action is
likely to provoke violence by others? At what point, again,
does picketing become violent? How far, in short, can resistance to an alleged injustice legitimately extend? Presumably,
it is all a matter of degree.

Where taxes are imposed which are allegedly inequitable,
or where the money so extracted from the population is put
to purposes of which individuals disapprove, I should have
thought that a Christian is entitled to protest, and to exert
all the influence he can muster to get the law changed, but
meanwhile should pay up – for a citizen's duty to pay taxes
is explicitly emphasized in the New Testament. Only in the
most extreme circumstances would he be justified in refusing
to pay and going to prison instead – for any widespread action
of this sort would lead to chaos and anarchy. But there are
other examples of unjust laws to which obedience should certainly be refused, whatever the consequences (although we
must always remember that this is very easy to say, but
exceedingly hazardous and costly to put into practice). An
obvious example of such disobedience would have been to
harbour a Jew liable to arrest in Nazi Germany. But individual
resistance to the law is likely to have very little effect. It is
only when resistance can be organized on a considerable scale
that the governmental shoe really begins to pinch.

Ever since Gandhi was so successful in his struggle against
the British Raj in India, there has been an understandable
vogue for the doctrine of 'passive resistance'. It must be recognized, however, that Gandhi owed an enormous debt in this
respect to the fact that the middle-class conscience in Britain
already had a certain sense of guilt about past imperialism,

and would never have countenanced the suppression of passive resistance by the naked use of force. It is doubtful how long Gandhi himself would have lasted had the British Raj been replaced by Hitler's Germany, Stalin's Russia or even considerably less extreme alternatives. It is true, of course, that, whatever may happen to the leaders, a general strike would comparatively soon bring any government to its knees, just as the boycott of buses organized by Martin Luther King forced a change in local legislation. But whereas such a boycott could be organized even in the 'Deep South' of the United States, it would be exceedingly hazardous, and might prove impossible, to organize a widespread withdrawal of labour, or campaign of passive disobedience, in a police state.

But this question of a just cause does not rest only on the fact that every means short of physical violence must first have been attempted. It turns also on the degree of injustice concerned. Here, again, we are up against a difficult question of definition, but one on which recent international conventions may, perhaps, throw some light. Thus the European Convention on Human Rights of 1950 made an attempt to give a more precise content to what the Universal Declaration of Human Rights, 1948, had termed 'the inherent dignity' and 'the equal and inalienable rights of all members of the human family' (after first stating unequivocally, in its Preamble, that 'it is essential, if man is not to be compelled to have recourse, as a last resort, to rebellion against tyranny and oppression, that human rights should be protected by the rule of law'). These minimum human rights were summed up in the ensuing Convention as the right to life (except in defined circumstances);[1] to freedom from subjection to torture, inhuman or degrading treatment or punishment,[2] or to slavery, servitude or forced labour;[3] to liberty and security of the person;[4] to a fair trial;[5] to freedom from retroactive criminal laws or punishments;[6] to respect for private and family life, home and correspondence;[7] to freedom of thought, conscience and religion;[8] to freedom of expression, peaceful assembly and association;[9]

[1] Art. 2.   [2] Art. 3.   [3] Art. 4.   [4] Art. 5.   [5] Art. 6.
[6] Art. 7.   [7] Art. 8.   [8] Art. 9.   [9] Arts. 10 and 11.

to an effective remedy against officials who violate these rights;[1] and to the enjoyment of all these rights 'without discrimination on any ground such as sex, race, colour, language, religion, political or other opinion, national or social origin, association with a national minority, property, birth, or other status'.[2] It is true that Article 15 provides that 'In time of war or other public emergency threatening the life of the nation any High Contracting Party may take measures derogating from its obligations under this Convention to the extent strictly required by the exigencies of the situation, provided that such measures are not inconsistent with its other obligations under international law'. But even when such derogation is admissible in principle, it is expressly provided that this must not extend to torture, inhuman or degrading punishments, slavery or servitude, *etc.*[3]

What this amounts to is that a State can scarcely be regarded as 'unjust', in the sense commonly accepted today, simply because it does not grant universal suffrage or tolerate an official opposition. There are, in point of fact, comparatively few countries in the contemporary world where true democracy prevails. It is only where a government can rightly be described as tyrannical that a violent revolution might, in principle, be justified; and the term tyrannical should, I submit, be reserved for régimes under which whole groups of people, and sometimes whole races, are treated as sub-human, or at least where palpable infringements of the rights defined by the European Convention are not only commonly perpetrated, but no effective means of redress is provided.

FOUR EXAMPLES OF CIVIL STRIFE

This whole subject may, perhaps, be brought into focus by a few practical illustrations. Take, first, the civil strife which exists today in Northern Ireland and in Eritrea. There can be no doubt that the Roman Catholic minority in Ulster were, until recently, the victims of palpable injustice through adverse discrimination and the deprivation of civil rights, and that they had ample justification for making their protest. But it seems clear that the Stormont government has gone a

[1] Art. 13.   [2] Art. 14.   [3] Art. 15 (2).

long way to remedy these injustices, and that acts of violence are now, at any rate, being perpetrated chiefly by the Irish Republican Army and their supporters, on the one hand, and sometimes by extreme Orangemen, on the other. The aim of the former is no longer (if it ever was) the relief of social injustice, but the unification of Ireland against the will of the majority of the inhabitants of Ulster. This is a matter of politics rather than social justice, in regard to which I can see no justification for violence; for Ireland can only properly be reunited by persuasion and mutual consent. The acts of violence committed by the extreme Orangemen are also politically inspired, represent an amalgam of prejudice and fear, and are equally, in my view, unjustifiable. Similarly, the revolt in Eritrea, like the troubles in Ireland, is a combination of politics and religion, for it represents the revolt of the mainly Muslim population of the lowlands against the Amharic rulers of Ethiopia. There is little doubt that they have genuine grievances, although it seems clear that these have been fermented, to some degree, from abroad; it is most unlikely that they have any real prospect of obtaining substantial reforms by constitutional means, at least for the present; but I am distinctly doubtful whether their grievances are sufficiently serious to justify the hardship and misery to which their armed resistance, and the severe reprisals from the government which these provoke, give continual rise.

Another criterion which is applicable to both the 'Just War' and the concept of a 'Just Revolution' is the means used and the extent of the suffering which is likely to be caused. And here it is relevant to observe that a campaign of passive resistance may, in some circumstances, cause more widespread suffering than a short and sudden outbreak of violence. A valid distinction can, moreover, sometimes be made between the sabotage of public utilities, or even any destruction of property, and acts which endanger life and limb. There is a lot of difference, too, between the comparatively small loss of life which may be unavoidable in a quick *coup d'état*, and the widespread butchery of a civil war or unrestricted guerrilla activities. There may be occasions when it is permissible to blow up a train which is transporting ammunition, petrol or some other commodity which is essential to military operations, even at the risk that the engine driver and guard may be killed or injured – or, indeed, to attack service personnel or others actively engaged in suppression; but there can be no justification for planting bombs which are likely to cause an indiscriminate loss of life among ordinary citizens.

Yet again, the criterion of the probability of success is equally relevant, for this is another major factor in balancing the weight of human suffering involved in rebellion, on the one hand, against that inherent in enduring continued tyranny, on the other. There is all the difference in the world between a sudden, well-planned movement to overthrow a tyrannical régime in which there is every prospect of swift success, and the inauguration of a guerrilla struggle which may go on for years and is probably (or very possibly) doomed to ultimate failure. In this assessment the likelihood of outside intervention is, of course, one highly relevant factor: as in the maquis, for example, in occupied Europe, when the resistance movement could always look forward to the expected invasion by the Allied armies. But on this criterion guerrilla activity in South Africa – to turn to another contemporary situation – could scarcely be regarded as morally justified at the present, for the prospect of success would appear minimal and the likelihood of effective foreign intervention remote. But it must be remembered, in this sort of context, that sophisticated societies can be very vulnerable, in some circumstances, to simple weapons, and that it is exceedingly difficult to bring armed might effectively to bear upon an enemy who knows how to use suitable terrain. It is also noteworthy that even unsuccessful rebellions have sometimes led, with the passage of the years, to the acceptance of the principles for which they were fought. It can scarcely be denied that there are circumstances in which the violent revolt of people toiling under the burden of intolerable oppression, however hopeless they may be of success, may bear the most eloquent testimony to the dignity of man and the stark tyranny which has driven them to the ultimate sacrifice.

On these criteria, it seems to me, no-one outside South Africa has the right to pass any facile judgment on those 'non-whites' who feel themselves driven to armed opposition to a manifestly tyrannical régime. I could not, myself, regard their action as morally justifiable, since I do not approve of some of their methods and can see no prospect of early success; but I feel compelled to regard their position as less culpable than that of the government whose oppression has driven them, at least in their view, to such extremes. The racial discrimination to which they are subjected, the cruel injustices inherent in indefensible legislation and ruthless executive action, the progressive closure of all avenues leading to reform and social change by constitutional methods, together with the inadequacy and ineffectiveness of pressures exerted from outside, clearly constitute what many regard as a wholly intolerable situation. But even this cannot be said to justify unrestricted violence or to remove the moral obligation, however agonizingly difficult this may be, to assess the human suffering entailed by the passive endurance of gross injustice, on the one hand, or by a revolt which must almost certainly be deemed premature, on the other. But however little anyone outside South Africa has the right to sit in judgment, it would, I think, be highly irresponsible to give those inside the country who feel driven to active opposition any *encouragement* to resort to violence, for this would not only amount to fighting vicarious wars but virtually to incitement to suicide. Outside sympathizers would be much better employed in the attempt to exercise an international pressure which is more effective, insistent and costly than anything we have yet seen.

Much the same sort of considerations apply, today, to the conflict between the 'Establishment' and the revolutionaries in Brazil. What is the duty of the corporate church, or indeed the individual Christian, when placed between a tyrannical government and a revolutionary movement? It is small wonder that the Roman Catholic Church is sharply divided on this issue, and that the minds and consciences of many other Christians are deeply perplexed. It is in the context of such situations that the Roman Catholic Bishops of England and Wales, in their 'Statement concerning Moral Questions' on 31 December 1970, asserted that 'It will not do merely to condemn the use of violence against authority, since evidently

D

those in authority may themselves be guilty of worse violence in the legislation they enforce . . . It is obvious that in some cases citizens can never obtain justice by peaceful or democratic means.' So it is not possible 'to issue a blanket condemnation of all who under any circumstances resort to violence. Where protests against injustice have been stilled by promises of redress which remain unfulfilled, it is governments who bear the heaviest responsibility for violence which may thus break out'. Having said this, however, they add a weighty *caveat* when they continue: 'Nevertheless, it remains true that civil violence can have such tragic consequences that a Christian may well think that it can rarely if ever be proportionate to the good that may be achieved. The logical consequence of civil violence is civil war. The bitterness between brothers, the scars and hatred left by civil war, remain for generations – much longer than the memories of international wars.'

This brings us to the last basic criterion for any 'Just Revolution': the confident hope and expectation that the revolutionaries will be able to establish a régime which is more equitable, and more consonant with the public interests, than the one they have overthrown. It is precisely at this point that writers such as Jacques Ellul deny that violence can ever have truly beneficial results. The first law of violence, he tells us, is continuity; for when 'once you start using violence, you cannot get away from it'. Similarly, the second law of violence is reciprocity, for '*all* who take the sword will perish with the sword'. Violence, he asserts, always 'creates violence, begets and procreates violence'. And in somewhat the same vein he insists that the third law of violence is sameness; for 'it is impossible to distinguish between justified and unjustified violence, between violence that liberates and violence that enslaves . . . Every violence is identical with every other violence. I maintain that all kinds of violence are the same.'[1] But this is not only much too doctrinaire; it simply is not true – particularly when one realizes that Jacques Ellul uses the term 'violence' to include any sort of force, psychological as well as physical. On a literal interpretation of this view it would be impossible for any government to fulfil its God-

[1] J. Ellul, *Violence*, pp. 94–97.

given duty to maintain law and order, for all government must rest to some extent on coercion as well as consent. Nor is it true to history to assert that a revolution *never* has salutary results, for he would be a bold (or singularly obtuse?) individual who would deny that the overthrow of the Nkrumah régime in Ghana, for example, was not beneficial to the people of that country and also marked by a minimum of bloodshed and suffering.

All the same, the fact remains that many revolutions have overturned one régime only to establish another, no less unjust and tyrannical than the one it replaced. Those previously oppressed have taken the opportunity to wreak their vengeance on their former oppressors; there has, indeed, been a reversal of roles; but the rule of law, and the reign of social justice, have been as conspicuous by their absence as they were before. The flag of liberty has been hoisted, high-sounding slogans have been bandied about, but the situation in fact remains as reprehensible as it has always been. This is, of course, understandable enough, and very human; but there can, for the Christian, be no justification whatever for a revolution of this sort.

And this is, indeed, one of the hallmarks of a great deal of the revolt, or spirit of revolt, which seems to characterize many movements of the extreme left today. There is a positive obsession – understandable enough, within limits – with the iniquities of contemporary society; there is a determination to explode the values, and undermine the foundations, of what is depicted as a false and evil system; but there is no clear conception of any viable alternative. Those who follow this line of thought dedicate themselves – often with the most single-minded and sacrificial devotion – to the work of destruction, but their ideas are essentially negative. When the evil has been eradicated, they believe, then something better must inevitably take its place. But this is a singularly barren, and even myopic, attitude. To the Christian, at least, it savours far too much of the man in the parable out of whom one devil was cast, but no positive power for good accepted in its place – with the dismal result that he was eventually possessed by seven devils, each worse than the first.

This means that the Christian must grapple with this whole subject of what seem to him unjust laws, and even tyrannical governments, with a combination of boldness, restraint and modest expectations which it is singularly difficult to achieve. His primary duty is to reach all men with the liberating message of the Good News in Jesus Christ – the message of a full and free forgiveness for the repentant sinner, whatever the evil and tyranny of which he has been guilty, and of a reconciliation between man and God which leads to a reconciliation between man and man, whatever the enmity and bitterness of their past relations. But he also has a duty to witness not only to God's love for individual men and women, but to his will for society as a whole; to demonstrate a God-given passion for social justice, and to denounce injustice with the fearless and uncompromising intolerance of the Old Testament prophets: in a word, to love his neighbour not only 'in word or speech but in deed and in truth'.[1] This means that his protest against evil and injustice, and his championship of the oppressed, must be costly to the point of genuine self-sacrifice. How very few of us get anywhere near this standard.

Yet with this boldness there must go a marked restraint. It is not that loving one's neighbour as oneself may not sometimes necessitate organized opposition to evil, for it well may. It is not that it may not ever lead to civil disobedience, or even – in some circumstances – to support for, or participation in, a revolution. Unless one is a convinced pacifist, it may even involve armed force. Nor could I, for one, *absolutely* exclude the permissibility, in extreme circumstances, of what may be termed tyrannicide; for I could not, for example, condemn Bonhoeffer, formerly a convinced pacifist, for his conviction that Hitler was so evil, and so deeply stained with innocent blood, that he had no option but to participate in a plot to destroy him. But each and every step down such a dark and slippery slope must, for the Christian, be characterized by a soul-searching restraint. In so far as his own interests are concerned, it is incumbent on him to suffer violence rather than to inflict it, for he is under an obligation to follow in the footsteps of his Lord. And even where his brother is concerned,

[1] 1 Jn. 3:18, RSV.

his protest should, wherever and whenever possible, be by persuasion rather than compulsion, by constitutional action rather than civil disobedience, by peaceful methods rather than violence. It is all too easy to reach a point where our reaction to injustice is emotional and instinctive, rather than reasoned, principled and controlled. It should, I think, be axiomatic for the Christian that he never breaks the law unless he feels compelled to do so, and that he never resorts to violence if there is any viable alternative. It can never be right to break the law of the land except in obedience to a higher law; and violence is always evil in itself. The Christian can never, therefore, resort to violence except as a deliberate choice of one evil as the only possible alternative to a greater.[1] And when faced by such a choice he would do well always to remember Cromwell's plea: 'I beseech you, in the bowels of Christ, think it possible you may be mistaken.' In particular, no human being has the knowledge, insight and utter moral integrity to embark on the treacherous waters of vengeance. It is not for nothing that it stands written: 'Justice is mine, says the Lord, I will repay.'[2]

THE 'THEOLOGY OF REVOLUTION'

Nor is it only this haunting sense that it is all too easy to embark on a course of political action which is mistaken, or even positively wrong, which must give rise to the modest expectations which, I have suggested, should be the third component in the Christian's approach to any attempt to redress injustice by passive or active resistance. A still more basic reason will be his fundamental conviction that it is not primarily by political action that the kingdom of God will be established. It is at this point that I, for one, must decisively part company with those contemporary theologians of whose teaching it has been justly remarked that 'Instead of showing the relevance of revelation to revolution, it makes revolution its source of revelation. The result is a secular gospel whose dominant emphases parallel those of Marxism'.[3] It is thus that a popular

[1] See pp. 54, 95f., *etc.* above.   [2] Rom. 12:19, NEB.
[3] 'Revolution and Revelation' by C. René Padilla, in *Is Revolution Change?* edited by Brian Griffiths (Inter-Varsity Press, London, 1972), p. 80.

preacher such as Colin Morris can write: 'So the prophetic mantle of Jesus passes to Marx, Lenin, and Mao, and then on to Castro, Ho Chi Minh, and Torres. But none is entitled to wear it for long. Each has his time of creativity and inspiration, and millions are rescued from oppression and hunger as a result. Such times pass; success destroys the revolution and the struggle must begin again.'[1] In his interpretation of Jesus, Colin Morris has, of course, fallen under the spell of a distortion of the Gospel records perpetrated by S. G. F. Brandon,[2] who sees in Jesus a leader of the Zealot movement whose political insurgence against Rome was the sufficient explanation of his crucifixion.[3] It is scarcely surprising, then, that Morris, for all his passionate and moving championship of the oppressed, ends his book with the lame remark: 'At any rate, even if my theology is all hay-wire, surely the man who fights for the rights of mankind to be human has a pretty strong claim upon God's mercy?' But this is no gospel at all. It is poles apart from the dynamic message of God's love and grace manifested in a full and free forgiveness through the atoning death of the Son of God (in which, it seems clear, neither Brandon nor Morris really believes) and in the new life and power bestowed by a risen Lord.

It is in somewhat the same vein that Joel Carmichael believes that Jesus' greatest moment of triumph was his 'seizure and occupation of the temple in Jerusalem', when he 'drives out the priests, the merchants and holds the Roman garrison (*sic*) in check . . . Jesus is the head of an organised movement against Rome and against those Jews who are traitors to their country';[4] and that Albert Cleage writes: 'Jesus was the colored leader of a colored people carrying on a national struggle against a white people . . . The activities of Jesus must be understood from this point of view: a man's effort to lead

---

[1] C. Morris, *Unyoung, Uncoloured and Unpoor* (Epworth Press, London, 1969), p. 151.

[2] S. G. F. Brandon, *Jesus and the Zealots* (Manchester University Press, 1967).

[3] This thesis, never at all convincing, has been amply refuted by Oscar Cullmann in *The State in the New Testament* (SCM Press, London, 1957).

[4] 'L'Épée de Jésus', in *Nouvelle revue française*, 1966 (quoted in English by Jacques Ellul, *Violence*, p. 47).

his people from oppression to freedom.'[1] Among the theologians, moreover, Harvey Cox clearly believes that God is preeminently present in political events, in revolutions and in upheavals.[2] More moderately, Richard Shaull insists that 'The God who is tearing down old structures in order to create the conditions for a more human existence is himself in the midst of the struggle . . . In this context, the Christian is called to be fully involved in the revolution as it develops. It is only at its center that we can perceive what God is doing . . . From within this struggle we discover that we do not bear witness in revolution by preserving our purity in line with certain moral principles, but rather by freedom to be *for man* at every moment . . .'[3] Again, Father Cardommel asks: 'How shall we observe Lent nowadays? By making, each of us, a revolutionary rupture with a society based on injustice, and by paralyzing the death mechanism of the money system – if necessary, by the well-planned general strike. Such is the Lent that pleases God, the Easter liturgy of today.'[4] And Father Maillard goes so far as to say: 'If I noticed that my faith separated me by however little from other men and diminished my revolutionary violence, I would not hesitate to sacrifice my faith. . . . The Christian as such does not interest me. I care only about the man who shows his concern for his brothers on a global level. If he truly wants to save mankind, we shall solve the problem of means together.' Authentic love, he tells us, 'comes through political, economic, sociological studies. We must love man on the level of his social betterment.'[5]

It is not in this way that the New Testament depicts the coming of the kingdom of God. None of these writers I have quoted seems to have any understanding of the basic sinfulness of human nature – the poor as well as the rich, the

[1] *Le Monde*, January 1968 (as quoted by Ellul, *op. cit.*, p. 48).
[2] Harvey Cox, *God's Revolutionary World* (SCM Press, London, 1969), pp. 20f.
[3] 'Revolutionary Change in Theological Perspective', in *Christian and Social Ethics in a Changing World*, edited by John C. Bennett (SCM Press, London, 1966), pp. 33 f.
[4] Conference on the Gospel and Revolution (22 March 1968), quoted by Ellul, *op. cit.*, p. 49.
[5] Quotations from *Frères du Monde*, taken from Ellul, *op. cit.*, pp. 56ff.

oppressed as well as their oppressors. Of course we should proclaim, with fearless conviction, the social justice God demands. Of course we should be prepared ourselves to suffer violence, if need be, for this end – and even in some cases, it may be, to resort to violence against intolerable oppression. But we must never, as we have seen, regard violence in itself as anything other than essentially evil, as never better than an awesome choice of the lesser of two evils. Nor must we for one moment imagine that to relieve the oppressed and to reform society – although that is, in fact, part of our duty – can make any basic change in the self-centredness of human nature. It is only that inward transformation that Christ alone, through his Spirit, can effect which can do this; and even then the old nature continues to struggle against the new. Our hope is not to make this world into a paradise, or to establish the Kingdom, for this we can never do. It is not to extirpate evil, for that will not happen till the King himself intervenes in judgment. Our object, rather, is to do the will, in our age and generation, of the One who went about doing good; who healed the sick and fed the hungry; who denounced pious hypocrisy and always called sin sin; and who died to reconcile sinful men to a holy God. Our aim is to make this world a place in which both God's love and his righteousness are displayed, and in which his gospel can be preached with meaning and effect. But the more fearlessly we stand for social justice, the more credible our message of the need for individual repentance and forgiveness will be.

5 MORALITY AND GRACE

In the second chapter of this book I began by giving some consideration to the nature of the society in which we live and its attitude to moral standards and ethical imperatives, and then to the nature and basis of these imperatives themselves. The moral standards of different races and cultures certainly betray considerable variations; and similar, if less radical, fluctuations can be observed in a single race or culture at different periods in its history. Do the moral imperatives on which these standards are based also vary, then, from age to age and country to country, and are they to be regarded as purely relative? Or is there a basic morality which rests on a more solid foundation than the changing customs of different cultures or succeeding generations, a morality which may be said to befit man as man?

In my third chapter I was primarily concerned with the relationship between morality and law – in Islam, in Hinduism and in contemporary jurisprudence in the West. We saw that it is sadly possible for positive law, on the one hand, to outrage moral standards, and thus to incur men's censure as unjust, despotic or even unworthy of the name of law; and that there are many moral precepts, on the other, which by their very nature cannot (and others which for one reason or another should not) ever be enforced by legal sanctions. But we also saw that morality cannot dispense with law in the regulation of human conduct, and that the law could not maintain its hold on men's allegiance if it were not reinforced by moral imperatives.

MORALITY AND RELIGION

It has, moreover, frequently been asserted – and almost as often denied – that there can be no morality without religion. Certainly it must be conceded that there has always been a very close connection between morality and religion, and that there is no religion worthy of the name which does not concern itself, in some measure at least, with the way in which its adherents conduct their daily lives – or, in other words, with their moral standards. It is also clear that men and women, all down the centuries, have habitually turned to religion both to provide the basis for their moral standards and the motive which prompts them to attempt to live accordingly. But it is equally obvious that atheists and agnostics are often men with high moral principles; so the question inevitably arises as to how far morality is, in fact, necessarily dependent on religion. Here, as it seems to me, three different aspects of such alleged 'dependence' should be distinguished.

a. The source and content of morality

First, we must consider the source and content of the moral imperative itself. It is undeniable that the source of this imperative has very frequently been found in the dictates of religion: that is, in what men have accepted as divine revelation. Thus we saw in my third chapter that the followers of the strictest school of Islamic orthodoxy believe that man can never discern the moral quality of human actions except in the light of the revelation which God has himself provided; and that it is meaningless even to talk of some actions as intrinsically good and others as inherently evil, since virtue and vice depend solely on what God has commanded or forbidden. Other Muslims, it is true, assert that the reason why God commands some things and forbids others is because they are, essentially, either good or evil; and that man can sometimes discern this fact even apart from revelation. In such cases, therefore, they hold that divine revelation may be said to confirm and reinforce a moral judgment which man might have reached by the exercise of his reason; whereas, in other cases, no human understanding would suffice and man is entirely dependent on what God has revealed.

Somewhat similarly, in Old Testament Judaism, morality is based not only on the Decalogue but on the moral precepts of a God-given law and the inspired teaching of the Prophets. In Hinduism, too, the concept of *dharma*, or duty, is regarded as based on the Veda and those later books which Hindus regard as inspired. In Buddhism, on the other hand, it may be questioned how far Gautama's 'enlightenment', and his subsequent teaching regarding the Four Noble Truths and the discipline to which they lead, is regarded as actually constituting divine revelation, for the various schools of Buddhist thought would differ on this point. Some of them put their faith in the intervention of supernatural beings (both Gautama and other 'Living Buddhas' and Bodhisattva), while others would emphasize the enlightenment which Gautama, as a man, himself achieved and then endeavoured to pass on to others.

But, however this may be, most humanists in our society today tend to find the basis for their moral teaching in some form of Utilitarianism. Naturally enough, those who adopt this general approach to morality differ among themselves not only in matters of detail but in the way in which they interpret what Utilitarianism really means; but it is, I think, sufficient for our purpose to say that their standard of reference is basically the promotion of human happiness or the diminution of human suffering. Everything which can be shown to promote the greatest happiness of the greatest number, or to reduce the sum total of human suffering, is right; and everything which militates against the greatest happiness of the greatest number, or induces greater suffering, is wrong. This may be expressed in simple terms of pleasure or pain or in the more sophisticated terms of the 'promotion of intrinsically excellent states of affairs, namely, personal relations and the appreciation of beautiful objects'. It is clear that this demand that all moral precepts should be tested by reference to the extent to which they 'further recognisable human ends' may, moreover, act as what D. M. MacKinnon terms a 'powerful dissolvent of entrenched moral beliefs based on the *ipse dixit* of traditional authority'.[1] But it must be remembered that Utilitarianism never professes to provide a complete system of morals; that many of its conclusions are wide open to question and debate; and that, whatever may be said of traditional morality in general, most of the moral imperatives of the New Testament can be justified even on utilitarian arguments. It is also clear that there may well be excellent grounds, however dimly we can discern them, for those moral principles which some Utilitarians would challenge.

When we turn to the further question which I discussed in my third chapter – the extent (if any) to which morality should be enforced by the law – it is interesting to note that some writers distinguish 'two sorts of morality, a morality of "universal values" whose acceptance is a necessary corollary of the viability of any society; and a morality of personal ideals which are essentially a matter of individual choice and are not susceptible of rational discussion'.[2] And while it is admitted that religious beliefs may influence a man's moral attitudes, any morality so affected is firmly relegated to 'the realm of the non-rational, the sacred precincts of personal belief, the personal "Answer", even personal idiosyncrasy'.[3] But this classification ignores any middle category of moral precepts which may not, indeed, represent a 'necessary corollary of the viability of any society' but which are, none the less, capable of rational commendation to the forum of public opinion as represented by the legislature.

But Utilitarianism is not the only basis on which men construct a theory of ethics which need owe nothing to religion. An alternative basis can be found in the views of those who may be described as Intuitivists. Again, of course, there are considerable differences in the way in which different writers expound their views, but the basic concept is that we all of us *know* that certain things are good and others bad and have an immediate apprehension of certain moral obligations. H. A. Pritchard expresses this conviction when he states that 'This

---

[1] D. M. MacKinnon, in *A Dictionary of Christian Ethics*, edited by John Macquarrie (SCM Press, London, 1967), p. 351.

[2] *Cf.* Basil Mitchell, *Law, Morality and Religion*, p. 104.

[3] Louis Henkin, 'Morals and the Constitution: the Sin of Obscenity', *Columbia Law Review*, 1963, vol. 63, p. 393 – as quoted by Mitchell, *op. cit.*

apprehension is immediate, in precisely the same sense in which a mathematical apprehension is immediate, e.g. the apprehension that this three-sided figure, in virtue of its being three-sided, must have three angles. Both apprehensions are immediate in the sense that, in both, insight into the nature of the subject directly leads us to recognise its possession of the predicate. . . '.[1] This is, in a sense, a development of G. E. Moore's insistence that there *is* such a thing as goodness, and we know what we mean when we use this term; but that the quality of goodness, though capable of apprehension, is beyond our definition. Thus he asserts that 'Everyone does in fact understand the question "Is this good?" When he thinks of it, his state of mind is different from what it would be, were he asked "Is this pleasant, or desired, or approved?" It has a distinct meaning for him, even though he may not recognise in what respect it is distinct. Whenever he thinks of intrinsic value or "intrinsic worth" or says that a thing ought to exist, he has before his mind the unique object – the unique property of things – which I mean by "good".'[2] Or, again: "If I am asked "What is good?" my answer is that good is good and that is the end of the matter. Or if I am asked "How is good to be defined?" my answer is that it cannot be defined, and that is all I have to say about it. But disappointing as these answers may appear, they are of the very last importance.'[3]

When we turn to what is often called the 'Emotive Theory', we find a flat denial that the statement that something is good means anything more than that the speaker approves of it. Thus C. K. Ogden and I. R. Richards assert that ' "good" is alleged to stand for a unique, unanalysable concept. This concept, it is said, is the subject matter of Ethics. When so used the word stands for nothing whatever, and has no symbolic function. This peculiar ethical use of "good" is, we suggest, a purely emotive use. Thus when we use it in the sentence "*This* is good" we merely refer to *this* and the addition of "is good"

[1] H. A. Pritchard, *Moral Obligation* (Oxford University Press, London, 1949), p. 4.
[2] Quoted from *Principia Ethica* (Cambridge, 1903), by Mary Warnock in *Ethics since 1900* (Oxford University Press, London, 1960), p. 27.
[3] Quoted, *loc. cit.*, p. 22.

makes no difference whatever to our reference. When, on the other hand, we say "*This* is red", the addition of "is red" to "*this*" does symbolise an extension of our reference, namely to some other red thing. But "is good" has no comparable *symbolic* function: it serves only as an emotive sign expressing our attitude to *this*, and perhaps evoking similar attitudes in other persons, or inciting them to actions of one kind or another.'[1] Similarly, A. J. Ayer insists that ethical judgments 'have no objective validity whatsoever' and that the function of all 'normative ethical symbols' (such as 'good' or 'wrong') is purely 'emotive', *i.e.* designed to express the speaker's feelings or to arouse those of the one he addresses.[2]

Much more could, of course, be said on this subject. But, however unfashionable this may be, I find myself unequivocally on the side of those who base their ethics on metaphysics rather than any theory of utility or intuition (although there is no reason that I can see why the conclusions about practical morality reached by those who approach the subject from any of these viewpoints should not, in many cases, coincide). As for A. J. Ayer's approach, I must confess that this always seems to me to result from a doctrinaire analysis, or exercise in abstract reasoning, which I find singularly unconvincing. With all those who advocate what may be termed 'Metaphysical Ethics', it seems to me virtually impossible to come to any satisfying conclusion about either the source or the content of moral imperatives until we have first considered such basic questions as the nature of the universe in which we live, man's place in this universe, and the meaning and purpose of human life. Only so can we come to any meaningful conclusion about what sort of behaviour befits man as man, or the still more fundamental question whether there is not in fact a God who not only created man but had a purpose in view when he did so; and whether he may not have indicated, in one way or another, what I have already referred to as the 'Maker's instructions' about how his creatures can best fulfil

[1] C. K. Ogden and I. R. Richards, *The Meaning of Meaning* (Routledge and Kegan Paul, London, 10th edition 1949), p. 228. *Cf.* also Mary Warnock, *op. cit.*, pp. 84 f.
[2] A. J. Ayer, *Language, Truth and Logic* (Victor Gollancz, London, 1956), p. 108. But *cf.*, in this context, p. 55 above.

their destiny (or, in other words, come to their own most complete fulfilment through living in the way that their Creator intended them to live).

How, then, can man come to any firm conclusion on this subject? Some Christians have maintained that morality is virtually identical with 'Natural Law', and that this, in its turn, can be perceived by man's unaided reason. The universe, they would say, was so created as to obey certain fundamental laws or principles; and man, who in a special way shares God's 'image and likeness', was created a rational creature who can understand something, at least, of the physical laws which govern the universe and of the moral laws which should regulate human beings in their individual and corporate lives. On this view, the divine law or revelation in the Old and New Testaments did not fundamentally affect the *content* of morality, although it 'spelt it out', so to speak, reinforced its authority and added certain specific precepts – and some Christians would argue that it is only the morality which can be justified by human reasoning, rather than by divine revelation alone, which should be enforced (and then, of course, with due regard to all the circumstances and considerations which I discussed in my last chapter) in a pluralistic society. And while it seems to me clear that Roman Catholic writers, in particular, have tended to give the concept of Natural Law a detail – and, indeed, a basis – which is both exaggerated and mistaken, we have the authority of Paul himself for the statement that those who know nothing of the revelation of the Mosaic law on Sinai yet 'show that what the law requires is written on their hearts, while their conscience also bears witness and their conflicting thoughts accuse or perhaps excuse them'.[1]

But, however this may be, it is clear that those who accept the fact of divine revelation will expect to find in that revelation either specific moral commands or at least principles on which moral conduct should be based – and that this will not only determine for them the source, but also the content, of those moral imperatives according to which they seek to direct their lives. Even so, there are, of course, many differences among

[1] Rom. 2:14, 15, RSV.

Christian writers about how they regard both the Mosaic law and even the moral precepts in the New Testament – and to this I shall return later in this chapter. Here it is, I think, sufficient to observe that while the disciples of 'Situation Ethics', as we saw in my second chapter, are apt to reduce the whole of morality to the absolute imperative of love (and to regard all other moral teaching in the Bible as little more than 'guidelines' as to how love should *normally* be interpreted and expressed), I myself find convincing reasons for believing that this view is both inadequate and incorrect. It is inadequate because fallen man needs clearer moral guidance than one single rule which he is inherently unable (particularly in times of conflict and temptation) to interpret and apply. It is incorrect because Christ gave his disciples divinely authoritative ethical precepts which the apostles subsequently developed and applied, under the inspiration of the Spirit who was specifically sent to 'lead them into all truth' and 'teach them all things'.[1]

b. *The motive for moral living*

Secondly, then, we turn from the source and content of morality to the motive or inspiration which prompts men and women to try to put this morality into practice in their daily lives. And here, again, the influence of religion has been paramount. It is not, of course, that there can be no other motive or inspiration, for it is certainly possible for a Utilitarian to find an adequate reason for acting contrary to his natural instincts in his conviction that such action will promote the greatest happiness of the greatest number or diminish the sum total of human suffering; for an Intuitionist, in his instinctive feeling of moral obligation; or even for one who regards ethics as nothing more than a series of value judgments, in his personal conclusion, however this may be reached, that one course of action is 'better' than another. But it can scarcely be denied that man's motive for moral living may be greatly reinforced by a wide variety of religious convictions. Thus the Buddhist finds his inspiration to follow the exacting moral discipline of

[1] Jn. 16:13 and 14:26. For Situation Ethics – and also the problem where two 'absolute' principles come into conflict – see pp. 50 ff., 101 above.

the 'Middle Way' in his deep desire to attain Nirvāna, and
thus to be released from a long cycle of reincarnations.
The Hindu is fortified in trying to act according to the
dharma of his caste – or even the dictates of the *sanātana* or
eternal *dharma* – by his belief in the law of *karma*, according
to which a man always reaps, in some future incarnation,
what he sows in this present life. Again, the Muslim finds
his inspiration to obey the Sharī'a in the thought of both the
penalties and rewards of the Day of Judgment; while Muslim
mystics, like Hindu *bhaktis*, find their primary inspiration in
the love of a personal God. And precisely the same is true of
the Jew or Christian, who is continually prompted to act in a
way from which his lower nature shrinks, or against which it
even rebels, both by the fear and, still more, by the love of
God. It is obvious, moreover, that this motive or inspiration
is not necessarily dependent on the truth of the religious beliefs
from which it springs, but rather on the conviction with which
these beliefs are embraced by the individual concerned.

c. The power for moral living

The situation is very different, however, when we come, in
the third place, to the *power* which enables men and women to
conduct their lives in accordance with those moral principles
which they cannot, of themselves, put into practice, however
hard they try. Clearly, the verbal distinction between this
heading and the last is merely a matter of semantics; but the
point I am trying to make is the difference between a motive,
or even a psychological inspiration, for moral conduct, on
the one hand, and an enabling which is more than psychological, and can only be explained in terms of a power which
comes to a man from outside his own resources, on the other.
Yet I am not thinking here of any experience in which a man
is not in control of his own actions – in the way in which this
is true of the mystic, for example, when in a state of ecstasy.
On the contrary, I am referring to a power which works inside a man, enabling him both 'to will and to do' what he would
otherwise neither desire nor be able to accomplish. Yet he
knows that this power, though it finds its expression in his
own thought, will and action, does not have its origin in his

own resources, but comes to him from outside himself –
whether in answer to prayer or as a spontaneous manifestation of divine grace. And here, of course, the validity – rather
than the intensity – of his religious convictions is vitally important; for all depends not on his psychological motivation
and inspiration, but on the reality, beneficence and power of
the God to whom he turns in his need.

MORALITY AND GRACE

This brings us, inevitably, to the heart of this chapter, the
relationship between morality and grace. To this our consideration of the relationship between morality and religion was,
I think, a necessary preliminary, since grace is essentially a
religious concept. It is often defined as 'free unmerited favour'.
In the Bible it is made abundantly clear not only that man
could never earn or deserve the love of God, but that the
very idea of his needing to do so is a hideous distortion. Jesus
himself said that if we, for all our evil, know how to give good
gifts to our children – not because they deserve them, or
because we *ought* to behave like that, but because it is natural
for a parent to love his children and desire their greatest
good – then how much more can we rely on the love of him
from whom all fatherhood in heaven and earth gets its
name.[1] So he told the story of the father whose love followed
his wayward son in his wanderings, watched earnestly for his
return, and welcomed him with a love which was truly
'prodigal'. In the Gospel, the 'prodigality' of the love of God
is shown most of all, of course, in all he has done, and all it
has cost him, to put away the sin which constitutes the only
barrier to the fellowship for which he always longs. This is
grace – the spontaneous manifestation of the love of God in
action. We have already used the term in relation to the
divine power which can – and does – strengthen our moral
weakness and so enable us to live on a plane to which we
could not otherwise aspire. But the inter-relationship of
morality and grace is far more fundamental than this. Indeed,

[1] *Cf*. Lk. 11:13 and Eph. 3:15. This is not in any way to obscure the fact
that we become sons of God, in the intimate family sense, only by what the
New Testament terms 'adoption' or 'new birth'.

the concepts often appear to be virtually contradictory, and to sum up two elements, in almost all religions, which seem to be in conflict and to compete for men's allegiance: the conviction that man must somehow work out his own salvation by the quality of his ethical achievements, on the one hand, and the conviction that he can never do this, but is utterly dependent on a salvation which is provided by God alone, on the other.

a. *In other religions*

An outstanding example of the former of these two concepts – namely, a 'salvation' (if, indeed, we may properly employ that term) which must be achieved by man himself – can be found in the Theravāda form of Buddhism, or in Zen-Buddhism today. A Theravādin is one who follows the 'Doctrine of the Elders', and it is the Theravāda branch of the Buddhist faith which, almost certainly, most accurately reflects the teaching of Gautama himself. The essence of his 'Enlightenment' was the solution he found to the problem of suffering, which he had come to regard as the basic characteristic of human experience. He perceived that 'the root cause of the universality of suffering was desire'[1] – the will to live and the will to possess – and that the only escape is first by resolving to have done with all such craving and attachment to the transient, and then by practising the eightfold discipline, moral and mental, of what he termed the 'Middle Way' (between, that is, the way of desire and attachment, on the one hand, and the extremes of asceticism, on the other). By faithfully following this discipline a man may hope, in some future reincarnation, to attain to the passionless peace called Nirvāna. And Zen-Buddhists, who put a paramount emphasis on a particular system of self-discipline, differ from this chiefly 'in positing an enlightenment or intuitive grasp of truth not only at the end of the Path, but here and now, as they persevere in the Path itself'[2] – or, in other words, in this present life rather

---

[1] *Cf.* E. O. James, *Christianity and Other Religions* (Hodder and Stoughton, London, 1968), p. 78.
[2] H. D. Lewis and R. L. Slater, *World Religions* (C. A. Watts, London, 1966), p. 76.

than in some future incarnation. It is a matter of dispute among scholars today whether Gautama himself really believed in a Supreme Being at all; but, however this may be, there can be no doubt that his primary emphasis was on what man himself can achieve.

When, however, we turn to the Mahāyāna form of Buddhism, which is now far more widespread, we find Gautama regarded as 'the latest and greatest of a series of eternal Buddhas who had appeared on earth to spread the saving Dharma to suffering humanity'[1] – together with a whole series of mythical heroes or Bodhisattva who all succeeded in attaining perfect knowledge but yet, in imitation of Gautama's example, denied themselves the rest and joy of entering the state of Nirvāna in order to help mankind by their teaching and practice of the doctrine of the Middle Way. And in what is commonly called Pure Land Buddhism we find a primary faith in a Bodhisattva named Amitabha who, long ago, 'accumulated such a vast store of merit on his progress towards Buddhahood that he bestowed on all who trusted in him . . . an assured rebirth in his paradise far away in the western quarter of the universe by the simple device of constantly repeating "Hail Amida[2]-Buddha".'[3] This is given an enormous emphasis in Shinshu teaching (which is the version of Buddhism most widely accepted in Japan today), where faith in Amita's merit is regarded as the all-important condition for attaining eternal felicity.[4]

We find very much the same phenomenon in Hinduism, a religion with so many facets and so many different, and even contradictory, schools of thought that it represents in itself a whole galaxy of religious concepts. To the Hindu 'salvation' is essentially emancipation from the bonds of our present existence and the material universe – rather than from moral guilt – and the felt experience of immortality; and different strands of Hindu teaching prescribe a variety of ways in which this can be attained. Sometimes this is by way of *dharma*,

[1] E. O. James, *op. cit.*, pp. 81f.
[2] An alternative spelling of his name.   [3] E. O. James, *op. cit.*, p. 83.
[4] For a fuller discussion of all aspects of comparative religion discussed in these pages, see my *Christianity and Comparative Religion* (Tyndale Press, London, 1970).

or duty; sometimes by way of asceticism; sometimes by way of knowledge; and sometimes by way of devotion. A Hindu may, in fact, interpret his religion in terms of polytheism, monism, monotheism or even atheism. There can be little doubt that the primary emphasis in most of the philosophical schools of Hindu thought has been on how man can himself achieve the emancipation (*moksha*) to which reference has already been made; but glimpses of the concept of a saviour-god continually appear, particularly among the *bhakti* sects.

In Zoroastrianism we find a major emphasis on the importance of both ceremonial and moral purity in this world in the light of the judgment of the world to come, with its punishment for the wicked and its reward for the righteous. In Islam, too, a primary place is always given to the Sharī'a, or sacred law, which prescribes in the minutest detail those commands and prohibitions which Muslims regard as the divinely revealed blue-print for the life of the individual Muslim – and, indeed, the Islamic State – here on earth. But in Zoroastrianism there is an expectation that before the end of the world three supernatural saviours will appear, each of them descended from Zoroaster. And the last of these will, with his assistants, slaughter an ox, and from the fat of that ox 'prepare Hush, and give it to all men. And all men become immortal for ever'.[1] Any such concept would, of course, be totally alien to Islam (especially in its Sunnī, or 'orthodox', manifestations); but even here there is a belief that, in the final issue, a man's salvation depends on whether the Almighty Judge will, or will not, extend to him his sovereign mercy – together, I think, with a popular conviction that, if a man recites the Muslim creed from his heart and is careful to observe the prescribed duties of prayer and fasting, he may, indeed, have to enter the Fire for a time, but will ultimately attain Paradise through the timely intercession of Muḥammad.

b. In the Bible

But it is time for us to return to the teaching of the Bible. And here it has been all too common for men to make a sharp dis-

[1] *Cf*. R. E. Hume, *The World's Living Religions* (T. and T. Clark, Edinburgh, 1959), p. 217.

tinction, or even postulate an antithesis, between the Old and the New Testaments. Under the Old Covenant, it is often asserted, salvation was to be attained by man through what we may term morality, or the divine law, while under the New Covenant salvation comes by way of grace alone, and must be accepted by the empty hand of faith. But this represents a caricature of true biblical teaching. It is certainly true that in the Old Testament there is a primary emphasis on law, and in the New Testament on grace; but this does not mean that the fundamental way of salvation under the Old Testament revelation was not always by grace – however this may have been misunderstood and perverted – or that the moral law does not also assume a place of great importance in the pages of the New Testament.

We can, I think, most conveniently examine this question in the light of Jesus' statement, as recorded in Matthew's Gospel: 'You must not think that I have come to abolish the Law or the Prophets; I have not come to abolish them but to complete them. Indeed, I assure you that, while Heaven and earth last, the Law will not lose a single dot or comma until its purpose is complete';[1] and also in the light of Paul's statement in the Epistle to the Galatians: 'Thus the law was a kind of tutor to conduct us to Christ, when we should be justified through faith.'[2] Now what, precisely, do these two passages teach? We can, I think, best understand their meaning if we adopt, in this context at least, the analysis of the Mosaic law which we find in the *Thirty-Nine Articles of Religion* – and elsewhere – as comprising three main, and largely distinct, elements: the moral law, the ceremonial law, and the 'civil' law.[3]

First, then, the *moral* law – which we may venture to regard as covering what Jesus once described as the 'weightier demands of the Law',[4] and which largely consisted in what we would today term not so much law as morality, since a great deal of it was not susceptible to litigation or legal sanctions.

[1] Mt. 5:17, 18, J. B. Phillips.
[2] Gal. 3:24, NEB margin. I have developed the argument of the next few pages at greater length but in much the same way in a lecture on 'Law and Grace' which is now out of print.
[3] *Cf.* Article 7.   [4] Mt. 23:23, NEB.

This law, in its essence, is both eternal and immutable: necessarily so, for it is an expression of the character of God himself and of that righteousness which, alone, can measure up to the divine standards. So, just as God cannot and does not change, nor can his law. On the contrary, the moral law, as an expression of God's character, is in its very nature timeless, while, as an expression of his will for men and women, it is co-terminous with the history of humanity. It existed before the Fall; it stood from the Fall until Sinai; it was articulated in some detail in the Mosaic law; and its basic requirements have always been written on men's hearts.[1]

Then Christ came, and 'completed' this moral law in three distinct ways. First, he completed it by giving it a deeper and more exacting meaning; for he taught that the moral law is as much a matter of inward disposition, motive and desire as of outward deed and word; that it represents all-pervading principles of character and conduct rather than a code of specific commands and prohibitions. He completed it, too, by his own unswerving obedience to its precepts, and by epitomizing its very principles and spirit in his life and character. He did this, moreover, not only in his sinless life but also in his atoning death, in which he met, on behalf of others, the just demands of a law which had been broken. But it is important to notice that he also completed it by reinforcing its demands on his disciples; for he said that, unless they showed themselves far better men than the Pharisees and the doctors of the law, they could never enter the kingdom of Heaven.[2] And the apostles in their turn re-expressed and re-imposed this moral law on the Christian church, for the Epistles abound with commands, prohibitions and exhortations to this end. So the importance of the moral law for the Christian can scarcely be exaggerated.

Secondly, the *ceremonial* law – which, it is important to remember, represented, in essence, the way of grace. That was its purpose and import, although in the Pentateuch it took the form of law. Its basis is this: that, ever since the Fall, man has failed to keep the moral law, and is a sinner both in nature and act; and that sin always and inevitably separates him from

[1] *Cf.* Rom. 2:15.   [2] *Cf.* Mt. 5:20, NEB.

a holy God. But from the first God seems to have revealed a way back to his life and fellowship, and this was given detailed and meticulous adumbration in the ceremonial regulations of the Mosaic law. Thus the different courts and curtains of the tabernacle and the temple, with their manifold prohibitions, were intended to demonstrate not only that the sinner could not saunter into God's presence, but that there was, none the less, a welcome, for the penitent and obedient, through the blood of atonement and the water of cleansing. But these truths were all taught in picture language, like 'puzzling reflections in a mirror';[1] they were embodied in a code of detailed rules, in a very legalistic form; and they involved many human distinctions, such as that between Jew and Gentile, priest and layman. Essentially, then, the ceremonial law enshrined the way of grace, epitomized in the repentant sinner with his sacrificial lamb; but the outward form was that of law, and was stereotyped in the minutiae of the temple ritual.

Then Christ came. He came 'under'[2] the ceremonial law, and he himself observed it – although he disregarded and scorned the additions and circumventions devised by men. But the Baptist identified him at the very beginning of his ministry as the 'Lamb of God'[3]; and it seems clear that it was the prophetic vision of Isaiah 53, in particular, which dominated his own interpretation of his mission throughout his whole life, and especially on the eve of his passion. So at the Passover feast the Paschal Lamb was slain[4]; the curtain of the temple was torn in two from top to bottom[5]; and the ceremonial law had fulfilled its purpose. But it is important to notice, at this point, the difference between the moral and the ceremonial law. The moral law was fulfilled and completed in Christ's life and in his death, but he re-imposed its requirements on his disciples; the ceremonial law was not only fulfilled and completed in his person and work, but was thereby abolished. Type was henceforth to be replaced by antitype, shadow to give way to substance.

Thirdly, there is the *civil* law – that is, detailed provisions about crime with its punishment and proof; civil status, slavery

---

[1] i Cor. 13:12, NEB.   [2] Gal. 4:4.
[3] Jn. 1:29.   [4] *Cf.* i Cor. 5:7.   [5] Mk. 15:38, NEB.

and debt; and much else besides. These laws were for the temporal government of the nation of Israel – which was, indeed, God's chosen race, but was made up of very human and unruly men and women. This is the part of the Pentateuch which most closely resembles law in the modern sense; and some of its provisions, which do not seem particularly lofty to the Christian conscience, have close parallels in the Code of Hammurabi and other codifications of law which have come down to us from the ancient Middle East. It was God-given in the sense that he specifically allowed its promulgation and enforcement for the civil government of first a pastoral, and then an agricultural, community; but at the same time it often fell far short of the moral law. An obvious example of this is provided by the Mosaic provisions for divorce, of which Christ observed that for man's 'hardness of heart' Moses had allowed this, 'but from the beginning it was not so'.[1]

Then Christ came, and completed the 'civil' law too.[2] How so? I think he himself gives us the secret in his application of the parable of the vineyard, in which the tenants not only rejected and maltreated all the landlord's messengers, but even murdered his son. Turning to the Jewish leaders, he declared: 'Therefore, I tell you, the kingdom of God will be taken away from you, and given to a nation that yields the proper fruit.'[3] So the people of God today no longer constitute an earthly nation for which specific laws of human government must be prescribed; instead, there is found among all nations the company of those who are redeemed and regenerate, on whom the moral law as such is divinely incumbent, but who are governed in such matters as crime, civil status, contract, *etc.*, by the positive law of the countries in which they live – the relationship between which and morality I have discussed, to some extent, in my third chapter. Thus the civil law in its Mosaic form has also fulfilled its task.

Secondly, and much more briefly, we must consider the meaning of Paul's statement that 'the law was a kind of tutor to conduct us to Christ'. I think that this is true in three distinct

[1] Mt. 19:8, RSV.
[2] In the sense that it had no longer any role to fulfil. See below.
[3] Mt. 21:43, NEB.

ways. First, in the sense that the moral law convicts us all of
sin: of commandments we have transgressed, and of standards
we have failed to achieve. So it brings home to us our need for
forgiveness (that is, for grace) as our only hope. The ceremonial law, moreover, always pointed the repentant sinner to the
promises of grace – but grace in the semblance and shackles of
law. So that, too, was designed to lead to Christ and his cross,
where grace stands fully revealed. But Israel as a whole
stumbled, both before and after Christ's coming; and, instead
of being driven by the moral law to take refuge in grace through
the provisions of the ceremonial law, the Jews erected out of
the moral and ceremonial law together a false way of self-
righteousness. So they missed the basic purposes of both, and
refused to submit themselves to the way of 'righteousness'
which God had revealed.[1]

Again, the moral law reveals not only our transgressions
and failures, but the essential sinfulness of the human heart.
So it drives us to regeneration (that is, to grace) as the only
remedy. It is not only that we have failed to keep the moral
law and are utterly unable to attain the standard it has set;
all too often we have not even wanted to keep it, and have
positively rebelled against its precepts. So we need not only
forgiveness but cleansing; we need a radical change in our
innermost beings. In this way, too, it conducts us to Christ.

Yet again, the moral law continues to reveal our failure and
sin even after we have experienced regeneration; so it goes on,
day by day, conducting us to Christ that we may find not
only renewed forgiveness but also sanctifying power (that is,
grace). This was typified in part, under the Old Covenant, by
the 'laver', or basin for ritual washing, in the ceremonial law,[2]
and was certainly apprehended by faith in such passages as
Psalm 51. But chiefly, even in the Old Testament, this cleansing and change of heart were depicted as characteristic
of the New Covenant which was to come;[3] for this New Covenant was not only to expunge past defilement, but to substitute
for an external commandment, graven on stone and demanding
our unwilling obedience, a law which is written on both heart

[1] *Cf.* Rom. 10:1–3.   [2] *Cf.* Ex. 30:18–21, *etc.*
[3] *Cf.* Je. 31:31ff.; Ezk. 36:25ff.

and mind – signifying the glad response to its dictates by one in whose will, affections and outlook God has done, and is doing, his sanctifying work.[1] So we feel compelled, again and again, to turn to Christ – for 'what the law could never do, because our lower nature robbed it of all potency, God has done: by sending his own Son in a form like that of our own sinful nature, and as a sacrifice for sin, he has passed judgement against sin within that very nature, so that the commandment of the law may find fulfilment in us, whose conduct, no longer under the control of our lower nature, is directed by the Spirit'.[2]

No wonder, then, that Paul says that 'Christ means the end of the struggle for righteousness-by-the-Law for everyone who believes in him',[3] and that the very purpose of the law was to be a 'kind of tutor to conduct us to Christ', that we might be 'justified by faith'. But what, precisely, does justification by faith really mean? It is clear from the New Testament teaching which we have already examined that this does not mean that the moral law is no longer incumbent upon the Christian. What justification by faith means is that the believer is first *accepted as righteous* (which is the sense in which Paul normally uses the word 'justified'), however deeply he may have fallen into sin, when he looks away from himself to his Saviour in self-abandonment and trust; and then that God begins to change both his inward disposition and his outward conduct, so that he is also *shown to be righteous* (which is the sense in which the word 'justified' is used in the second chapter of the Epistle of James[4]), by the way in which he acts and behaves.

This does not mean that we attain salvation by a sort of combination of morality and grace, that we half receive it as a gift and half earn it by the way in which we behave. On the contrary, the New Testament teaches that salvation is entirely through Christ, not man; entirely through grace, not morality; entirely through faith, not achievement. But it also teaches that what has been termed 'saving faith' is much more than mere mental conviction, for it constitutes, as we have seen, a

---

[1] *Cf.* Heb. 8:10.
[2] Rom. 8:3 and 4, NEB.
[3] Rom. 10:4, J. B. Phillips.
[4] *Cf.* Jas. 2:31, 24, *etc.*

radical turning away from ourselves, both in our sin and in our efforts to earn forgiveness, and an abandonment of our past, present and future – our guilt, our lives and our confidence – to the One who died for our sins, who rose again for our justification, who ever lives both to intercede for us and to make his home in our hearts, and who will finally take us to himself.

It is, I think, in the light of this supreme revelation of what God has done, is doing and has promised to do that we can best understand the wistful longings for a saviour-god, and even the mythological stories of such a god's intervention, which we find in so many different religions. Of these faint and fitful glimpses of man's need and God's grace (as of the authoritative pictures and prophecies of the Old Testament) it may justly be said that in Christ and his cross they find their perfect fulfilment. He offers a salvation unequivocally based on grace, not morality, which is wide open to the most debased of men, and need only be accepted by the empty hand of faith; but he also calls his disciples to the highest standard of ethical living – and makes available to them a supernatural grace which, alone, can enable them to respond.

BIBLIOGRAPHY

(*This is not a reading list, but is confined to books to which reference has in fact been made in the text or footnotes.*)

Adams, Jay E., *Competent to Counsel* (Presbyterian and Reformed Publishing Co., Philadelphia), 1970.

Anderson, J. N. D., *Christianity and Comparative Religion* (Tyndale Press, London), 1970.

Anderson, J. N. D., *Christianity: the witness of history* (Tyndale Press, London), 1969.

Ayer, A. J., *Language, Truth and Logic* (Victor Gollancz, London), 1956.

Barclay, William, *Ethics in a Permissive Society* (Fontana, London), 1971.

Barry, F. R., *Secular and Supernatural* (SCM Press, London), 1969.

Bennett, John C. (editor), *Christian and Social Ethics in a Changing World* (SCM Press, London), 1966.

Board of Social Responsibility of the General Synod of the Church of England, *Civil Strife*, 1971.

Board of Social Responsibility of the General Synod of the Church of England, *Obscene Publications: Law and Practice*, 1970.

Brandon, S. G. F., *Jesus and the Zealots* (Manchester University Press), 1967.

Campbell, C. A., *Selfhood and Godhood* (George Allen and Unwin, London), 1957.

Cox, Harvey, *God's Revolutionary World* (SCM Press, London), 1969.

Cullmann, Oscar, *The State in the New Testament* (SCM Press, London), 1957.

Devlin, P. A., *The Enforcement of Morals* (Oxford University Press, London), 1965.

Dworkin, Gerald (editor), *Determinism, Free Will and Moral Responsibility* (Prentice-Hall, New Jersey), 1970.

Ellul, J., *Violence* (SCM Press, London), 1970.

Fletcher, J., *Situation Ethics* (SCM Press, London), 1966.

Ginsberg, M., *On Justice in Society* (Penguin Books, Harmondsworth), 1965.

Griffiths, Brian (editor), *Is Revolution Change?* (Inter-Varsity Press, London), 1972.

Guntrip, H., *Mental Pain and the Cure of Souls* (Independent Press, London), 1956.

Haldane, J. B. S., *Possible Worlds* (Chatto and Windus, London), 1945.

Haldane, Robert, *Epistle to the Romans* (Banner of Truth Trust, London), 1958.

Hart, H. L. A., *Law, Liberty and Morality* (Oxford University Press, London), 1963.

Hook, Sidney (editor), *Determinism and Freedom in the Age of Modern Science* (New York University Press), 1958.

Hume, R. E., *The World's Living Religions* (T. and T. Clark, Edinburgh), 1959.

Huxley, Aldous, *Ends and Means* (Chatto and Windus, London), 1937.

James, E. O., *Christianity and Other Religions* (Hodder and Stoughton, London), 1968.

Keeling, Michael, *Morals in a Free Society* (SCM Press, London), 1967.

Keeling, Michael, *What is Right?* (SCM Press, London), 1969.

Lewis, C. S., *Miracles* (Fontana, London), 1967.

Lewis, C. S., *The Screwtape Letters* (Fontana, London), 1955.

Lewis, H. D. and Slater, R. L., *World Religions* (C. A. Watts, London), 1966.

Lunn, Arnold and Lean, Garth, *The New Morality* (Blandford Press, London), 1964.

Macdonald, D. B., *Muslim Theology, Jurisprudence and Constitutional Theory* (Charles Scribner's Sons, New York), 1903.

MacKay, D. M., *Christianity in a Mechanistic Universe* (Inter-Varsity Press, London), 1965.

MacKay, D. M., *Freedom of Action in a Mechanistic Universe* (Cambridge University Press, London), 1967.

MacKinnon, D. M. (editor), *Making Moral Decisions* (SPCK, London), 1969.

Macquarrie, John (editor), *A Dictionary of Christian Ethics* (SCM Press, London), 1967.

Mascall, E. L., *The Importance of Being Human* (Columbia University Press, New York), 1958.

Micklem, Nathaniel, *The Art of Thought* (Epworth Press, London), 1970.

Mill, J. S., *Utilitarianism, Liberty and Representative Government* (J. M. Dent, London), 1910.

Mitchell, Basil, *Law, Morality and Religion* (Oxford University Press, London), 1967.

Morris, C., *Unyoung, Uncoloured and Unpoor* (Epworth Press, London), 1969.

Mowrer, O. Hobart, *The Crisis in Psychiatry and Religion* (Van Nostrand Co., Princeton), 1961.

Ogden, C. K. and Richards, I. R., *The Meaning of Meaning* (Routledge and Kegan Paul, London), 1949.

Pritchard, H. A., *Moral Obligation* (Oxford University Press, London), 1949.

Rhymes, Douglas, *No New Morality* (Constable, London), 1964.

Robinson, J. A. T., *Christian Freedom in a Permissive Society* (SCM Press, London), 1970.

Robinson, J. A. T., *Honest to God* (SCM Press, London), 1963.

Rommen, H. A., *The Natural Law*, translated by T. R. Hanley (Herder Book Co., London), 1947.

Schaeffer, Francis, *The God who is There* (Hodder and Stoughton, London), 1968.

Streeter, B. H., *Adventure, the Faith of Science and the Science of Faith* (Macmillan, London), 1937.

Taylor, T. M., *The Heritage of the Reformation* (St Andrew's Press, Edinburgh), 1960.

Warnock, Mary, *Ethics since 1900* (Oxford University Press, London), 1960.

Way, Arthur S., *Letters of St Paul and Hebrews* (Macmillan, London), 1926.

Williams, Glanville L., *The Criminal Law* (Stevens, London), 1953.

Zaehner, R. C., *Hinduism* (Oxford University Press, London), 1966.